The local police com
with a locksmith wh
scene of carnage v
entered made the pol   .... y telegraph immedi-
ately to the Sûreté (the French equivalent, broadly
speaking, of Scotland Yard).

Monsieur Taylor, Chef de la Sûreté, and his assist-
ant, Monsieur Marie-François Goron, arrived with a
doctor.

There were three bodies. The first, that of the maid,
lay in the hall. She had obviously just come out of her
bedroom when she was attacked. In the bedroom she
had left, her young daughter, with whom she shared
the bed, had also been killed. In the main bedroom
sprawled Mme de Montille, her cambric nightgown
slashed to ribbons.

'All of them had their throats cut,' said the doctor,
'as well as sundry other wounds, inflicted with a very
sharp knife. The type butchers use.'

'This place reminds me of a slaughterhouse,' mut-
tered Taylor, looking round at the blood-spattered
walls of the apartment . . .

About the author

Douglas Wynn served in the RAF during and just after the Second World War. He then took a degree in Chemistry at London University and worked for some years as a research chemist before becoming a technical college lecturer. Retiring early he was able to concentrate on writing and his interest in criminology. An adult-education tutor in writing, he is also a member of the Society of Authors and the Crime Writers Association. He has written articles on his hobby and has a wide collection of books on the subject. This is his third book on true crime. The previous two were *Settings for Slaughter* and *Blind Justice?*

THE LIMITS OF
DETECTION

Ten of The World's Strangest Detective Stories

DOUGLAS WYNN

WARNER BOOKS

A *Warner* Book
First published in Great Britain in 1992
by Warner Books

A CIP catalogue record for this book
is available from the British Library.

ISBN 0 7515 0122 0

Printed and bound in Great Britain by
Richard Clay Ltd, Bungay, Suffolk.

Warner Books
A Division of
Little, Brown and Company (UK) Limited
165 Great Dover Street
London SE1 4YA

To Rosemary

Acknowledgements

For permission to quote from *Crimes That Shocked Australia* by Alan Sharpe, I am happy to thank the publishers Reed Books Pty. Ltd. And for permission to use material from *My Work At The Sûreté* by Commissioner Jean Belin, I am grateful to the publishers George G. Harrap & Co. Ltd.

Contents

Introduction

Dr Edmond Locard, a pioneer of scientific criminology in the French city of Lyons, once said that every criminal leaves something behind him at the scene of the crime – a piece of cotton, perhaps, from his clothes, a strand of hair from his head – and also takes something away. Potentially then the criminal can always be caught if we can detect the traces he leaves behind, or find anything that connects him with the scene of the crime.

Although there have been staggering advances in improving the sensitivity of scientific methods of investigation over the years, mistakes have also been made. Well-publicised cases like the Birmingham Six have shaken public confidence in forensic scientists. This is a pity because the application of these methods, by dedicated workers, owing allegiance only to the truth, can go a long way towards solving a crime, as will be illustrated in this book.

But scientific techniques are not the only weapon in the armoury of the crime fighter. In the past some police forces have used bizarre methods to track down criminals, as in the use of a psychic medium, which turned up useful evidence, but led to an unexpected twist in the case when it came to court.

Sometimes a detective solves a case by a combination of intuition and a large slice of luck. When a book fell open at a certain place it revealed the murderer's method – and sunlight striking across a page revealed secret writing to an observant policeman, in another case.

But in the main, difficult murders are solved by painstaking enquiry, eliminating everybody until you come to the murderer – what Colin Wilson has called the 'needle in the haystack' method. The detectives have to keep slogging away even when everyone else has given up and gone home. And there are some good examples of persistence in this book. The detective who captured mass murderer Landru, for example, showed dedication to the chase far above that which we would normally expect and followed it even in the face of opposition from his colleagues and his boss. Another policeman pursued his enquiries all over Europe only to discover that the man he was seeking was safely under lock and key in the detective's own town. And even then he turned out not to be the murderer. Finally, persistence under conditions of the most extreme cold, searching for clues hidden under a blanket of snow, brought to justice a multiple murderer in the Yukon and amply justifies the subtitle of this book: 'ten of the world's strangest detective stories'.

1

What's In A Name?

'Why are you getting up so early? Come back to bed, darling.' The woman turned sleepy eyes upon the naked man who had just crawled out from between the warm sheets.

As the faint light of dawn filtered through the shutters he could see her forty-year-old face, still showing traces of the paint and powder that she habitually wore.

The room was draped with red satin and the furniture was Louis XVI, very fashionable in Paris in the 1880s. The bed was of ebony with a large canopy over it and a tasselled bell-pull hanging down at the side.

The man was of muscular build, not particularly handsome, though he sported a fashionably luxuriant moustache. He shivered a little, for it was a cool day in March, and looked around for his clothes.

'I shall have to have some money, Marie.'

At once she sat up in bed. 'Don't call me that!' she snapped. 'My name is Regine.'

'Regine de Montille,' he laughed. 'Well, have it your own way. Although I believe you are better known as Marie Regnault. Seriously though, I'm right out of cash. Are you going to let me have a small loan?'

The woman lay back in bed and her eyes narrowed:

'You realise, of course, that many men pay, and pay handsomely, for spending the night here?'

'Yes, I know,' said the man in a tired voice. 'There's a rich broker in Paris who pays you a thousand francs a month, and an old gentleman who pays only four hundred. But I'm not old and I thought I was your lover.'

The woman reached over and helped herself to a small cigar from an ornate box on the bedside table. She lit it and looked at him through the cloud of smoke. 'You amuse me, my dear, and we've had some good times together, but I don't want a permanent lover. And I'm certainly not keeping you.'

The face of the naked man, sitting at the end of the bed, darkened. 'If you won't give me any money, Marie, I shall have to take some.' He looked at the safe, covered with black pearwood to resemble an ordinary piece of furniture and standing over against the wall between two windows. 'Or sell some of your very extensive collection of jewellery.'

His words jerked the woman up on the bed. 'Don't you dare!' she cried. 'I'll call my maid and send her for the police.' She reached out a hand for the bell-pull.

The man shrugged his broad shoulders, turned his back on her, and walked towards the chair where he had left his clothes.

Suddenly he turned. His face was contorted with the animal passion that a few hours earlier had stimulated her jaded appetites, but now forced a scream from her lips. In his hand he carried a large butcher's knife. She screamed again and her hand grabbed for the bell-pull, but the flashing blade was already swinging in a wide arc.

It was about seven in the morning when the cook banged on the concierge's door of the block of flats at 17, Rue Montaigne, Paris.

'I can't get any answer from Madame de Montille's flat,' she complained.

The caretaker went with her to try again, but the only sound from the apartment was the mournful howling of two dogs. The concierge sent for the police.

The local police commissary arrived later that morning with a locksmith who soon had the door open. But the scene of carnage which met their eyes when they entered made the police commissary telegraph immediately to the Sûreté (the French equivalent, broadly speaking, of Scotland Yard).

Monsieur Taylor, Chef de la Sûreté, and his assistant, Monsieur Marie-François Goron, arrived with a doctor.

There were three bodies. The first, that of the maid, lay in the hall. She had obviously just come out of her bedroom when she was attacked. In the bedroom she had left, her young daughter, with whom she shared the bed, had also been killed. In the main bedroom sprawled Mme de Montille, her cambric nightgown slashed to ribbons.

'All of them had their throats cut,' said the doctor, 'as well as sundry other wounds, inflicted with a very sharp knife. The type butchers use.'

'This place reminds me of a slaughterhouse,' muttered Taylor, looking round at the blood-spattered walls of the apartment.

'Been dead several hours, I would say,' continued the medical man imperturbably. 'But I'll be able to let you know more definitely after the postmortem.'

The other detective, Goron, meanwhile had been prowling round the bedroom. 'Looks as if the murderer stripped, either before or after committing the crime. There's an imprint here of a man's bare foot outlined in blood.'

The Chef de la Sûreté nodded his head. His face was very pale. 'You continue your investigation here,' he said to Goron. 'I'm going to round up some witnesses for the examining magistrate to interview.'

There was a slight smile on the young detective's face as he watched his squeamish boss leave the room. A few hours later he met him again, this time at the Quai des Orfèvres, in the office of the examining magistrate, Monsieur Guillot, who was officially in charge of the case.

The magistrate shuffled some documents, in a self-important manner, on his desk. 'Well, gentlemen, I think we've been able to establish the time of the murder, from the statements I've taken, without having to wait for the postmortem.' He searched through the papers. 'The concierge of the block of flats next door heard two terrible cries in the early hours of the morning, though she wasn't able to establish the exact time. But an employee of the Ministry of the Interior, whose room faces that of the maid, said that he awoke at five o'clock in the morning. Soon after, he heard a long cry, then what sounded like a child's scream. Thinking it was his own child he went to her bedroom, but she was sleeping peacefully. Another tenant, who lives immediately below Mme de Montille's flat, was awakened about six in the morning by someone coming down the staircase.'

'So what it amounts to is this,' summed up Taylor. 'The crime was committed about five this morning and the murderer made his escape as soon as the outside door of the block of flats was opened.'

'That's right,' said Guillot. 'The concierge opens the front door every morning at just before six o'clock to allow a tradesman to call on one of the tenants.

'We've also been able to establish,' he continued, again searching the pile of documents on his desk until he came to the right one, 'that a man called on Mme de Montille at about eleven o'clock last night. The concierge wasn't able to see him very clearly as the gaslight had been turned out on the staircase. He simply called out, "Mme de Montille", and went on up the stairs.'

Taylor turned to Goron. 'Have you anything to report?'

The young detective nodded respectfully. 'If I could first add something to what M Guillot has just said? Mme de Montille had two little pug dogs, but nobody heard the dogs barking during the night, which means that nobody broke in and committed the murders. If they had the dogs would have barked. The murderer must have been the man who called late, presumably stayed the night with Mme de Montille, and committed the crimes in the early morning.'

'Yes, yes,' said the Chef de la Sûreté. 'We realised that. Get on with what you found in the apartment.'

'Well,' said Goron, slightly put out that his reasoning seemed to be dismissed so easily, 'we searched the flat thoroughly and Detective Jaume found a detachable shirt cuff under Mme de Montille's arm.'

'Ah,' said Taylor, hitching his chair forward in interest. 'Anything else?'

'Yes, sir. Another cuff was found under the body of the maid. Then I came across a man's yellow belt. On the inside, written in Chinese ink, was the name "Gaston Geissler".'

'That's interesting,' said Taylor. 'Mind you, bearing in mind what sort of woman she was – did you notice the bowl of visiting cards in the hall, all of them from men? – perhaps it's not too surprising to find a man's belt and shirt cuffs in the flat.'

'Yes, sir. And when we wiped away the blood from the cuffs we found the same name, "Geissler", written inside.'

'Did you indeed?'

'And we also found a letter, presumably written to Mme de Montille, signed "Gaston" and dated the 14th of March – that's only three days ago – and the envelope was postmarked Paris.'

'We'll put out a general call for this man Geissler,' remarked Taylor decisively. 'Circulate all the hotels and lodging houses in the Paris area. There's only an outside chance that he's registered under his real name, but you never know, we might be lucky. We'd also better interview all those men who left their calling cards.'

'Have we established a motive yet?' enquired the magistrate, who felt that he was in danger of being left out of the discussion.

The Chef de la Sûreté drummed his fingers on the arm of his chair and looked at his young assistant.

'I think we can say it was robbery, sir,' said Goron. 'The cook says that some jewellery is missing. Although the murderer never managed to get into the safe, there are blood stains all over it. But luckily it has one of those new locks that can only be opened when turned to the correct number.'

'Have you a list of the jewellery stolen?' enquired Taylor.

Goron nodded. 'There's a large diamond ring, diamond earrings, a heart-shaped watch and some bracelets.'

'We'll circulate a list of the missing pieces to jewellers and to other police forces around the country in case our man decides to make a run for it,' said Taylor.

The following morning when young Goron reported for duty at the Quai des Orfèvres he found a note on his desk asking him to go and see his chief. There he was told that a man called Henri Geissler had registered at the Hôtel Cailleux.

Goron and Jaume raced over to the establishment, which was in Montmartre near the Gare du Nord. The proprietor however had bad news for them.

'He's gone,' he said, throwing out his hands in an

expressive gesture. 'Geissler arrived on the 5th of March. At the end of the week I asked for payment and he said he would pay me at the end of the next week. I warned him that if he did not I would put him out and confiscate his luggage. But he slipped out the night before last and I haven't seen him since.'

'The night of the murder,' muttered Jaume.

Goron nodded his head. 'Short of money, too.'

After obtaining a description of the missing man they examined his room. There was very little in it. A cheap valise stood in a corner and on a table by the window there was a pile of papers. While Jaume lifted the valise on to the bed Goron examined the table top. He found a jumble of old Paris newspapers, some parchment packets, which smelt as if they had contained cigars and bore the addresses of tobacconists in Cologne, a season ticket for the tramways in Vienna, and – because the hotel did not supply meals and residents usually brought in their own food – some pieces of pork wrapped in paper.

The young detective was about to turn away when he noticed that the paper in which the food was wrapped was not a newspaper but an election manifesto from the Socialist candidate in the German town of Breslau.

A shout from Jaume interrupted his thoughts. 'Here, look at this, chief.'

Goron turned to where the other detective was bending over the opened valise. Jaume handed Goron an ornate metal locket with, inside, the photograph of a woman in old-fashioned clothes. Next he fished out some loose shirt collars with the maker's name printed on the inside. 'Nadge, Mohrenstrasse, Berlin'.

'Looks like we're after a German,' said Goron.

His assistant was looking at some cheap shirts he had just pulled from the case. 'He registered here under the name, "Henri Geissler",' said Jaume slowly, 'but look at this.' He handed over one of the shirts.

There, on the inside of the neckband, written in Chinese ink, were the initials 'G.G.'.

'Gaston Geissler!' exclaimed Goron.

They went back to the Sûreté with their finds.

The case had created a sensation in Paris. The newspapers were full of the story and reporters followed the young Goron about knowing that he was the most senior detective actively investigating the crime.

On the following Monday a reporter called to see him at the Sûreté. The reporter slumped in a chair in a nonchalant manner. 'Well, I see you've solved the case,' he said.

Goron sat up in his seat. 'What are you talking about?'

'Don't try and be cagey with me!' laughed the reporter. 'The man you've just arrested in Marseilles, of course. Isn't he the murderer of Mme de Montille?'

The detective's mouth fell open. 'I don't know anything about a man arrested in Marseilles,' he protested.

'It's no use trying to pull the wool over my eyes! I've got independent sources of information.' He reached into an inside pocket and handed Goron a telegram. It had been sent by the paper's correspondent in Marseilles and reported that a man had sold some jewellery to prostitutes in the town. They had told the police, who found that the pieces were on the list of the jewellery stolen from Mme de Montille's apartment. They had promptly arrested the man, whose name was Pranzini, and were holding him.

Goron took the telegram to the office of his chief, who read it through while an angry look appeared on his face.

'Do you think it's true?' asked the young detective.

'Oh, yes,' said Taylor. 'The Marseilles police are like that. They're afraid we would steal their thunder. They'd sooner tell the newspapers first and us much later. I suppose I shall have to complain to the Prefect of Police here in Paris and he will have to get in touch with the Prefect in Marseilles who will then get in touch with the police commissioner there. Only then will we get proper official details of the arrest.'

'But do you think this Pranzini is our man?'

'What do you think?'

'Well,' said Goron slowly and thoughtfully, 'Geissler is undoubtedly a German and Pranzini sounds Italian to me.'

'Do you think there could be two of them in it?'

'Only one man called on Mme de Montille late that night and only one was heard coming down the stairs in the morning.'

'What might have happened,' said the Chef de la Sûreté slowly, 'was that Geissler did the murder and sent some or all of the jewels to Pranzini to sell in Marseilles. I'll make arrangements to have Pranzini brought to Paris, but I want you to get on Geissler's trail and hunt him down. Go to Germany if necessary, but I want him found.'

A short time later Goron received a report from the Brussels police. It concerned a young American lady who was spending a few days in Antwerp. She had recently met a man in the Place Verte who said his name was Geissler. He asked directions to the Red Star Line Shipping Company and seemed anxious to board a boat for America. They had coffee together in a café and the lady noticed that the man's hair was dyed. He confessed that he had recently fled from France where he had been in some terrible trouble and he tried to make her a present of some jewellery. He also had a deep gash on his hand which was bound up with a handkerchief. She helped him replace the dressing on his injured hand with a new one and when he'd gone realised that she still had the handkerchief. In the corner were the initials 'G.G.'. The lady, who had heard about the murder in Paris, immediately went to the police.

The young detective travelled to Brussels and went to the police station where the handkerchief was. On examining it, however, he quickly saw that the initials were not 'G.G.', but 'C.C.' and the confusion had arisen because they were in Gothic Script. Later in the day came a report from the Antwerp police that the man calling himself Geissler had been found and proved to be an elderly eccentric, well known to the police, who had made up the story just to ingratiate himself with the American lady. He obviously was not Goron's killer.

The dispirited detective took the next train for Cologne. Arriving in the early hours of the morning he reported to the police, then went to a hotel to get a few hours sleep. Later that day, in company with a German detective acting as interpreter, he began a round of the tobacconist shops in the town, while the Cologne police organised a search of hotels to see if a Geissler had ever stayed in them.

For Goron it was slow, tedious work and it was largely unsuccessful. The description of Geissler from the Hôtel Cailleux was recognised in only one shop and the girl assistant who recognised it had not seen the man for five weeks.

But at the end of the day, when the French detective went back to the German police station, the chief of police had good news for him.

'Herr Goron, I think we're on the trail of your Geissler.'

Detectives had discovered that a man of this name and description had stayed at the Hôtel de Europe from the 29th of January to the 2nd of February and had then left without paying his bill. But this promising trail rapidly petered out. The clothing left behind in the room looked nothing like the clothing at the Hôtel Cailleux. The man had also left an address in Bavaria, which turned out to be that of his father, and when the hotel management wrote to the father the correspondence showed that this Geissler could not have been in Paris at the time of the murder. Yet another trail had gone cold.

But all this only served to increase the young detective's determination to find the man. He journeyed on to Berlin, arriving to find the town deep in snow and a bitter wind blowing in the streets. But the welcome he received from the German police was warm indeed. They were most interested in the Socialist manifesto the man had been carrying, for the police considered that Geissler might be a dangerous political extremist. They therefore directed one of their best detectives to help Goron. He spoke French very well and accompanied the French detective to the Nadge shirt factory in the Mohrenstrasse. Goron was taken to see the director, Herr Nadge, who was an elderly man. In the director's office there were also three younger men, all acknowledged shirt experts.

After they had carefully examined the now clean collars for some time and discussed the situation between themselves, Herr Nadge spoke. 'I'm sorry, Herr Goron. Although these collars are undoubtedly ours, you must understand that we make so many that it is impossible to say who bought them. As to the shirts,' – he picked one up between the tips of his fingers as if he felt it might contaminate him – 'I can tell at a glance that it is not one of ours.'

He gave one shirt to each of the younger men and there followed an examination, of typical German thoroughness, punctuated with small expressions of distaste as each man commented unfavourably on the workmanship of the garments.

After some time and a hurried consultation between Herr Nadge and his assistants he made the expected pronouncement. 'These are not our shirts. I would say that they were made in the provinces.'

'Could you possibly give us an idea, Herr Nadge,' asked Goron, through his interpreter, 'where these shirts were manufactured?'

The elderly shirtmaker turned up his nose. 'I'm afraid I cannot. It could have been any one of half a dozen towns.'

'Which do you think is the most likely?' persisted the French detective.

Herr Nadge began to look impatient: 'I cannot help you. It could have been Dresden, Leipzig or even Breslau. They all have shirt factories.'

Breslau! That name again! Goron had intended to go on to Vienna from Berlin, but when the name of the German town came up again he thought he would try his luck there.

Since the Berlin police had been unable to trace a Geissler among their files of political undesirables, the young detective bade them farewell and took the train for Breslau. He arrived in the town – which is now in Poland, close to the border with Czechoslovakia – late at night, but nevertheless went to the central police station. They had been telegraphed to expect him and a detective, called Hoffman, who spoke good French, was detailed to accompany him to his hotel.

As they rode in the horse-drawn cab through the darkened streets Goron noticed a shop with its lights still on. He gazed idly through the shop window as they passed, then grasped the arm of his companion compulsively. There in the window was an exact replica of the valise he had found in Geissler's room in the Hôtel Cailleux!

They stopped the cab. Goron had been carrying the valise, together with its contents, in his luggage, all over Germany, and it was the work of only a few moments to unearth and take it with them to the leather goods shop.

The proprietor, who was just closing up, was none too pleased to see them, but readily agreed that Geissler's valise was identical to the one in his shop window. And he gave them some further information. The only manufacturer of that type of case was a factory here in Breslau. Goron went to bed that night feeling the fates were beginning to smile on him.

The next day he went to the central police station, where Hoffman greeted him. 'Ah, good morning, Herr Goron, I trust you slept well? I've put in hand enquiries at the valise manufacturer and we are running down every Geissler we can find in the town. And later we'll go round the various shirt factories together. I have a feeling your quest will soon be at an end!'

But several days later Herr Hoffman's optimism was somewhat dented. The valise manufacturer could not identify who had bought Geissler's case. The Breslau police had contacted all the Geisslers in the town and none of them had been away during the month of March. And Goron and Hoffman were having no greater success with the shirt manufacturers. The French detective was turning his thoughts towards Vienna when one morning Hoffman came into the office with his face flushed.

'Herr Goron, I've some good news and some bad!'

'Please tell me the good news first.'

'Very well,' said Hoffman with a smile. 'I've a man outside who recognises the shirts! He's a small manufacturer we seem to have missed up until now. But he definitely states that the shirts were made in his factory. And he can even tell us to whom they were sold!'

'Good Heavens, Herr Hoffman,' expostulated Goron, 'what can be the bad news?'

'Ah, well, that's as far as we can go. The shirts were sold to a woman called "Guttentag", not "Geissler". And he doesn't even know Frau Guttentag's address.'

'But you surely have a local directory? We can look up all the Guttentags, make a list and go and see them all.'

They finished with thirty-six addresses for Guttentags and later that day knocked on the door of the nearest one to the police station.

It was opened by an elderly female servant.

'Herr Isaac Guttentag?' enquired Hoffman consulting his list. And he produced his papers identifying himself as a police detective.

The elderly lady examined the documents closely. Then she said, 'I'm afraid the master is out and won't be back until later today.'

'It was really your mistress we wanted to see,' persisted Hoffman.

'You can't see her. She's travelling abroad.'

Hoffman consulted his list again. 'I believe there is a son?'

The servant shrugged her shoulders. 'I don't know where he is. He doesn't live at home.'

After Hoffman had translated these replies, Goron said, 'Ask her if she recognises the valise.'

The German detective showed the old lady the case and she again looked very closely at it. It was beginning to dawn on the two that the old lady was shortsighted. She handed it back. 'I don't recognise it,' she said.

The detective's shoulders slumped. Then on an impulse Goron reached into his pocket and brought out the locket with the photograph of the woman in old-fashioned clothes, which had been found in Geissler's room. He handed it to the German lady. She shook her head and was about to hand it back when she changed her mind and held it close to her face.

'Why,' she said, 'it's a picture of Frau Guttentag.'

A shiver went down the French detective's spine.

The elderly servant was able to identify the shirts and the collars, having washed them herself many times, as belonging to the son of the house, George Guttentag.

The father, Herr Isaac Guttentag, when he returned that night and met the detectives, confirmed their suspicions. An elderly Jew, he obviously viewed his son with disfavour.

'I have disowned him,' he said fiercely. 'I refused to tolerate his conduct any longer and he left here at the beginning of March. I've had no contact with him, but a cousin of his has had letters from him from Paris.'

Goron groped in the valise and took out one of the collars with the name 'Gaston Geissler' written on the inside. He passed it to Hoffman who handed it to the old gentleman. Guttentag held it up to the light for a moment while he gazed at the writing. Then he nodded his head.

'That is my son's handwriting,' he said.

Having obtained the address of the cousin the two detectives went to see him. He was far less antagonistic towards the errant son than the father had been.

'The poor chap may have had a few youthful indiscretions, but that was no cause to cut him off without a pfennig.'

He showed them the last letter he had received from Paris from George Guttentag.

It was in German and Hoffman, after briefly scanning it, gave the gist to Goron. 'He says that he was arrested in the early morning of the 17th of March as a result of attempted suicide and having no money or any home to go to.'

'My God! That was the night of the murder,' exclaimed Goron. 'Well, go on.'

'He was remanded for eight days.' Hoffman showed the French detective the letter. 'Look at the bottom.'

There at the bottom was an address for replies – 'Mazas' (a prison in Paris), 'First Division, Cell No. 85'.

Goron held his head in his hands: 'Here have I been running all over Europe looking for Geissler, or Guttentag, and all the time he's been lodged in prison in my own town and I didn't know about it! What a police force we have where the Sûreté is not informed of the arrests the rest of the police force make!'

'Presumably he would have been arrested under the name of Guttentag,' suggested Hoffman mildly. 'But there's something else in the letter. He says that he told the magistrate that he was waiting for money from his family in order to get back to Germany.'

Hoffman turned to the cousin. 'Did you send him any money?'

The man looked decidedly sheepish. 'I sent him two hundred and fifty francs,' he muttered.

'To come back here?'

The cousin shook his head slowly. 'I don't think he'll come back here. He'll go either to Hamburg or Bremen and take a steamer for America.'

'If we're not quick,' said Goron when this was translated for him, 'he'll slip through our fingers.'

Together they rushed to the telegraph office and sent a message to the police in Paris asking them to hold Guttentag on suspicion of murder. Then they went back to the police station in Breslau where the chief there cabled to Bremen and Hamburg giving a description of the wanted man and requesting that he be held if he tried to board a ship.

On the long journey back to Paris the French detective was on tenterhooks that he would arrive to find that Guttentag had again disappeared, but when he reached the French capital and dashed to the Mazas prison it was to find that the prisoner was still in Cell 85. Now that his mind was relieved he took his time before interviewing Guttentag and consulted the deposition of the policeman who had arrested the wet and bedraggled figure on the banks of the Seine after an apparent attempt at suicide by drowning.

As he glanced down the brief report, he stopped at a single sentence. And the bottom fell out of his world!

Guttentag had been arrested at five o'clock in the morning. But the murderer of Mme de Montille could not have left the block of flats until nearly six because the concierge did not open the main doors until that time. Guttentag could not have been the murderer.

When he finally saw the sullen German in prison he asked him why he had chosen the name 'Gaston Geissler'.

The man shrugged. 'When I reached Paris,' he said in halting French, 'I was at the end of my tether. I had no money, no friends here, no prospect of a job. I decided to do away with myself. But I didn't want to bring disgrace to my family so I changed my name. "Geissler" is a common name in Germany.'

'So you just chose the name out of the blue?'

'Certainly. I don't know anyone called Geissler.'

Goron went back to the Sûreté headquarters at the Quai des Orfèvres a very chastened man to report that Geissler wasn't the murderer of Mme de Montille.

'Oh, yes, I know that,' said his chief. 'Pranzini's obviously our man. We've found a cutler who remembers selling a butcher's knife to a customer answering his description. Then two young women came forward to say that Pranzini, whom they know, came to stay with them the day after the murder and he had bloodstains on his clothes. He spent the night with them – apparently he's quite a lad for the ladies – then left the next morning for Marseilles, leaving behind some jewellery which was on the list as having been stolen from Mme de Montille's flat. He also has injuries on his hands and thighs no doubt sustained in fighting with his victims. Incidentally, Pranzini's name was on one of the cards in the flat. But when we went to interview him he'd already decamped to Marseilles.'

The young detective sat down despondently. 'I seem to have spent my time on a wild goose chase.'

'Not at all,' said his boss. 'If you hadn't run down Geissler, in a most remarkable display of perseverance, and shown that he had nothing to do with the case, we'd have been in trouble when Pranzini comes to trial. His counsel would have pointed to this man Geissler and accused him of the crime. And we wouldn't have been able to prove otherwise. No matter how good our case was it might have at least sown enough doubt in the minds of the jury to allow Pranzini to get off. Oh, and by the way there's a chap outside waiting to see you.'

Goron took the man waiting to see him back to his own office and had a considerable surprise when the man spoke.

'My name is Gaston Geissler,' he said, 'and I've known Henri Pranzini for many years. He was born in Egypt of Italian parents and has always had a remarkable gift for languages, which unfortunately he has often used in the perpetration of frauds, mainly against women. Some years ago he was employed at the Royal Hotel in Naples as an interpreter and I also worked there, as a secretary. I was instrumental in having him

23

convicted of theft and he swore that he would get even with me.'

Goron nodded. This explained why there were so many clues to Gaston Geissler left in the murder apartment.

Pranzini was tried for the brutal murder of the two women and the child and found guilty. He was guillotined on 31 August 1887.

When M Taylor retired from the post of Chef de la Sûreté the following year, M Goron took his place.

2

A Slight Trace of Blood

Anna Eckel looked at the smashed door and an uneasy feeling swept over her. It had obviously been forced by some heavy implement being thrust into the space between the door and the jamb and levered until the wood splintered and the lock sprang open.

But why would anyone force their way into the room of her friend Lina Lindörfer? Anna could think of only one person and as the thought came she turned to gaze fearfully down the stairs she'd just come up. But there was no one looking up at her.

This, after all, was the house of Lina's elder brother Friedrich. Both of them were in their fifties but when Friedrich had taken over the farm and coopering business from his parents he had promised to give his younger sister a home for life because she was a cripple, having had a diseased hip since birth.

The house, standing at a crossroads just outside the little southern German village of Reichelshofen, was not large. Downstairs there was only a kitchen, living room and bedroom and these rooms were shared by Friedrich, his wife and two grown-up sons. Upstairs there were three rooms and an attic. Lina had two of them. One she used as a kitchen and living room combined and the other as a bedroom. The other room on that floor was occupied by Lindörfer's grown-up daughter, her husband and two small children. It was no wonder there were tensions in the overcrowded house. Lindörfer had been trying for years to get his crippled sister to move elsewhere, but in that remote rural region of Bavaria in 1962 accommodation was not easy to come by.

It was a warm evening in May when Anna Eckel, with a pile of clothes over her arm, walked from her own house in the village to the Lindörfers' and came upon the broken door. She pushed gently on the smashed woodwork. 'Lina,' she called, 'I've brought some sewing for you to do.'

There was no reply.

Anna pushed the door open wider and stepped inside. It opened directly into the kitchen and the table was laid for the evening meal, but there was no sign of the crippled seamstress. A sewing machine in the corner had a pile of clothes flung over it and this was unusual since Lina was a very tidy person.

Anna called out again to her friend and walked into the bedroom. It too was empty. She walked back into the kitchen and jumped with fright.

There, standing in the open doorway, was a grim figure. Gaunt, unshaven and wearing working clothes, the man glared at her fiercely.

'What do you want?' he snarled.

The woman shrank back. 'I only called to bring some sewing to Lina, Mr Lindörfer. But she's not here.'

'I don't want you poking about in my house!'

He stood aside as the frightened woman scuttled out of the room and stumbled down the wooden stairs.

Anna knew the lady who lived next door to the Lindörfers and to her she poured out her story.

The neighbour shrugged her shoulders when she heard of Lindörfer's rudeness. They both knew of his rough tongue. But she was intrigued by Lina's disappearance. 'That's funny,' she said. 'If Lina does go out she usually leaves a note pinned to her door saying when she'll be back.'

Sometime later the neighbour, who was rather braver than Anna Eckel, walked round to the Lindörfer house. She went straight to the workshop where Lindörfer was busy making a barrel and asked him outright what had happened to Lina and why her door was broken.

The neighbour's forthright manner plainly discomfited the cooper. 'I don't know anything about a broken door,' he muttered. 'I'll tell you this, though, it wasn't done before Anna Eckel got here.'

'That's ridiculous! Why would Anna break the door?'

'I don't know,' said Lindörfer. 'All I know is that Lina left here about two o'clock this afternoon. She got into a car with a man I didn't recognise and they drove off. I'd just stepped out of the workshop and saw them leave. But she didn't tell me where she was going.'

'Poppycock!' scoffed the neighbour. 'Lina would never go off with a strange man.'

'Oh yes she would. You know as well as I do that she was always writing to those matrimonial agencies that advertise in the papers. Maybe she found a husband at last.'

The neighbour turned away thoughtfully. It was quite true that Lina did correspond with several lonely-hearts societies and it was not unknown for her to meet and go out with men with a view to marriage. Perhaps she really had gone away as Lindörfer said.

But Anna Eckel, when this conversation was reported to her, was angry at Lindörfer's insinuation that she had broken the door and in retaliation she went to the police station in the nearest town, Rothenburg ober der Tauber. There she saw Police Sergeant Pfliegl.

'It's a slanderous suggestion of Lindörfer's, that I smashed the door,' she stormed. 'More likely he broke it himself and forced the poor woman to flee. I want it investigated!'

The sergeant sighed. It sounded like another domestic squabble to him. He knew the Lindörfers and was well aware of the overcrowded conditions in which they lived, although there were many families in the area who were similarly placed. He also knew that Friedrich had an unpleasant, truculent manner, but was nevertheless regarded by his neighbours as basically a decent, hardworking man, whereas Lina was sometimes thought of as an embittered spinster with an acid tongue.

Pfliegl drove to Reichelshofen. He inspected the door, which was still broken, and looked through Lina's rooms. Then he questioned Lindörfer himself. The cooper repeated essentially the same story he had told the neighbour. The police sergeant instructed him to write to all Lina's relatives and ask if she was staying with any of them. Then he went back to Rothenburg and later filed a missing-persons report with his superiors in Munich.

After several weeks, back came the instruction to check whether Lina had taken a substantial sum of money with her when she left. As a consequence of this, at the beginning of July, a party of police from Rothenburg descended on the house at Reichelshofen and made a search of Lina's rooms. They discovered a cash box containing savings-bank books, each of which showed a substantial deposit. In addition, no money had been withdrawn from the accounts for a considerable time. There was also a fairly large cash sum in the box.

Would Lina have gone away for an extended stay without taking much money and leaving her bank books behind?

On the 9th of July the case was assigned to the criminal division of the Bavarian State Police at Ansbach, the nearest large town to Rothenburg. Inspector Heberger was put in charge.

Assisted by Sergeant Klug he began by questioning the Lindörfer family again. Then they talked to all the neighbours and people in the village for whom Lina had done any sewing. No one had seen her since the 10th of May, the day Anna Eckel had called to see her.

Bulletins were sent to all missing-person centres in the states of West Germany and her description circulated to newspapers which published 'search' notices. The newspapers which had been delivered to Lina were collected and all the lonely-hearts advertisements in them listed. Then enquiries were made to see if she had answered any and what subsequently had taken place.

The police also began a search of the area surrounding Reichelshofen. Streams, lakes and rivers were all investigated, but no sign of the missing woman was found. And the missing-person search was similarly unsuccessful.

'It's a puzzling case,' said Heberger one day in late July to his assistant. 'Lina's sisters all say that feelings between Friedrich and Lina often ran high and he was always trying to get her to leave. He used to lock the woodshed so that she couldn't get firewood, leave her bicycle out in the rain and appropriate her part of the kitchen garden. They believe that he has done away with her and I think they might just be right.'

'Yes, but they don't live in the area,' argued Klug. 'All the evidence they have to go on comes from the few visits they made each year and what Lina told them. They only heard her side of the story.'

'That's true. But don't forget that no one else saw Lina leave but Lindörfer. And his evidence seems to change with time. He told Sergeant Pfliegl that he could not describe either the man she went off with or the car. Yet he told other people it was a green car. Then someone else heard it was yellow and still another that the car was grey.'

'He's confused, sir. He's just a thick country yokel.'

'He might be. But he could also be lying and can't remember what story he's told last. I think we'll concentrate a bit more on the Lindörfer house. See if we can find any evidence of a crime.'

Once again a team of policemen arrived at the house in Reichelshofen, this time with the intention of going through the whole place from top to bottom. They removed food from Lina's rooms and sent it for analysis to see if it contained any poison. They scanned every surface, looking for suspicious stains which might be blood. They took some of Lindörfer's trousers away and also some of his shoes and sent them to the forensic laboratory in Munich. They even removed the linoleum from Lina's room and sent that to be examined for bloodstains.

But the food contained no known poison; the clothes and the shoes were free of bloodstains and there was no detectable blood on the linoleum.

A few days after the results had come in, Sergeant Klug approached his boss. 'I've just been to a lecture by Dr Lothar Lautenbach of the Erlangen Institute of Forensic Medicine. He was talking about the detection of minute bloodstains.'

'I can't see what use that's going to be to us,' grumbled Heberger. 'We've been all over that house with a microscope almost. We couldn't have missed any blood.'

'Ah yes, but these scientists use things like a luminol spray. Makes the bloodstain glow in the dark. They can detect traces of blood invisible to the naked eye, and then transfer the minute amount to a glass rod for testing as to group and so on.'

'Well, I don't know, I'm beginning to believe that

Lindörfer might be innocent.' But after further thought he came back to Klug. 'We'll give it one last shot. I'll get in touch with the Director of the Institute at Erlangen and ask if he can give us any assistance. But if nothing comes of it I think we'll have to give up this case.'

The Director of the Forensic Institute gladly offered to help the police and asked Dr Lautenbach to take charge of the scientific work. At just after eight o'clock on the evening of the 29th of August, the forensic scientist, with his young assistant, arrived at the house in Reichelshofen. He was accompanied by Heberger and his men and also by the district attorney who wanted to see for himself how this new search for bloodstains was carried out.

The door was opened by Lindörfer, who was handed yet another search warrant. His face went quite pale at first, but he quickly regained his composure and treated the searchers with his usual indifference and truculence.

Outside in the street a crowd quickly gathered. There was a certain amount of muttering about the police, who seemed to have nothing better to do than to keep harassing peaceable citizens.

Lautenbach concentrated on surfaces which might be expected to show stains from bloody hands, such as doors and the jambs and knobs, stairs and stair rails, and sink taps. Then he examined places where a body could have been dragged, such as the floors and steps, and where blood could have been splashed, for example the walls.

The suspect area was sprayed with luminol and then illuminated with an ultra-violet lamp. If blood was present a blue fluorescence showed up under ultra-violet light. The test worked best in semi-darkness.

They found very little of significance downstairs. The party then moved on to the stairs leading to the first floor.

'We'll try here,' said Lautenbach, examining the wood carefully in the fading daylight, 'but I don't anticipate any positive results because, unless I'm very much mistaken, these stairs have been freshly painted.'

'That's correct, sir,' said Heberger. 'I questioned Mrs Lindörfer earlier and she admitted that she repainted them, and the stairwell, a few weeks ago, on the instructions of her husband. That was after Lina disappeared.'

'Hm,' said the district attorney. 'Suspicious to say the least. Well, let's get on.'

The party moved slowly and laboriously up the stairs and eventually entered the missing seamstress's rooms. Both were examined minutely, but not a trace of blood was discovered. Then, at last, another door on the landing was sprayed and there, about halfway up, appeared a small blue spot.

'Where does that lead?' asked the district attorney.

'To the attic, sir,' said Heberger.

Lautenbach cautiously opened the door. Beyond was a room covering the whole width of the house, but very short in depth. To the right a flight of steps led up into the roof space. The place was a chaotic clutter with some ancient chests, a broken wooden bucket, a pile of charcoal briquettes and a sink. Between these items was the usual collection of rubbish to be found in all attics.

Proceeding carefully into the room and spraying as he went the scientist discovered a patch of blue on one of the few places where the floorboards were exposed. It was quite a large patch, a foot and a half long by about six inches wide.

There came a gasp from behind Dr Lautenbach as the district attorney leaned over his shoulder. 'Is that blood?'

'Could be,' said the scientist cautiously.

'Then we might have found the place where the murder was committed! If there was a murder, of course,' he continued lamely as he realised he was jumping to conclusions.

Lautenbach said nothing, but continued to spray objects around the patch. Some bright blue spots appeared on the pile of briquettes and on the steps leading up to the roof space just above the bloodstained area on the floor.

'Blood could have been splashed up here,' muttered the forensic scientist. 'In which case it looks like a frenzied attack on a victim.'

'Carry on!' said the district attorney excitedly.

Dr Lautenbach continued his search and came across some more spots on an old pair of shoe trees and on some corrugated cardboard.

Sometime later, having found no more blue spots, he called a halt. 'I think that's as much as we can do for the moment. We'll photograph the room, then have that floorboard up and also shave the wood where we've come across spots on the door and steps. And these, together with the movable objects, I'll take back with me to Erlangen.'

'You'll let us have the results as soon as you can?' asked the district attorney.

A few days later the forensic scientist rang Heberger at Ansbach. 'It's been extremely difficult to character-ise the marks,' he began cautiously. 'There is so little to work on. The piece of floorboard, for example, had obviously been washed, scrubbed even, many times—'

'Still that in itself,' interrupted Heberger, 'shows that we are on the right track. Lindörfer has obviously gone to great lengths to remove incriminating evidence.'

'Yes,' replied Lautenbach drily, 'but we still have to obtain the evidence. We had to cut down into the wood between the grain in order to get enough material to test. But the charcoal briquettes were better. We obtained sufficient from them fairly easily. And the same applied to the cardboard. On the other hand the wood from the door and the steps was much more difficult.'

'Yes, yes, doctor. I'm sure it was. But what we'd all like to know – in fact we're all desperate to know here – is, are the stains blood?'

'Oh yes,' said the scientist. 'They are undoubtedly blood and human blood too.'

'Well, that's great! That's marvellous!'

'Now don't go off the deep end,' cautioned Lauten-bach. 'We still have to prove that the blood group is the same as that of the missing woman. And this is where we've run into real trouble. There simply isn't enough material from the floorboard to do adequate tests for blood grouping. It's the same with the other wood samples and the cardboard. We've been able to get sufficient from the briquettes to do the long series of tests we need to establish the group, but unfortunately there is something else in the briquettes which interferes. So, although I think that the blood group is A, I haven't been able to confirm it.'

'Still, that's something. I'll make enquiries to see if she had been into hospital and if they have a record of her blood group.'

'That's a good idea. Also see if there is any of her unwashed underclothing still around the house. We might be able to determine her blood group from bodily secretions.'

A few days later a pile of clothes from Lina Lindörfer's rooms was despatched to the lab at Erlangen. And from tests done there it was established that her blood group was indeed A.

Lautenbach now wrote a detailed report and suggested that what was needed was another search for bloodstains in the attic, to obtain enough material for the complete testing for blood group. Every object in the room should be examined. He apologised for being unable to be present at the search as he had to go away to attend an important conference, but promised that they would begin the examination of the fresh samples as soon as he returned.

When Dr Lautenbach returned from his conference

he went to see his assistant and asked him, 'Where are the samples from Ansbach?'

The young man went very red: 'I'm afraid there aren't any samples, Herr Doctor.'

Lautenbach frowned. 'Why not?'

The assistant coughed to clear his throat. It was clear that he was not finding it easy to speak.

The older man could see the difficulty his assistant was having. He drew out a lab stool and perched himself upon it, then motioned for the young man to do the same: 'Sit down a minute, my boy, and tell me what happened.'

'I think it was Thursday of last week. The district attorney came in here with his retinue and wanted to see our results. I showed him what we'd done and he started to question me.' Here the young man flushed again as the memory of what had obviously been a very unpleasant time came back to him. 'I suppose I didn't explain things very well. I could see that the district attorney was not satisfied. Possibly he felt that our findings were not good enough to stand up in court. Anyway he asked me to test the piece of floorboard again.'

'What did you do, the benzidine test?'

'Yes, Herr Doctor, but I couldn't get it to work! I kept getting a negative reaction. And eventually the district attorney said he wasn't satisfied we had proved a case.'

'Well, we all make mistakes. I'll have a word with the district attorney myself.'

But the eminent Dr Lautenbach could not persuade

the official to change his mind. The lawyer was mindful that the only real evidence they had against Lindörfer was the forensic evidence, which was so slender it might be torn apart by a good defence counsel, should the case ever come to court. He had therefore decided to abandon the investigation.

There was no more that the scientist could do. He had no standing in the overall investigation of a crime. That remained the province of the police or the district attorney. He was simply a specialist assistant.

He was therefore somewhat surprised to receive a letter, some six months later, in the spring of 1963, from an Inspector Valentin Freund. The inspector had recently been transferred from Munich to Ansbach, had a good grounding in science and fully appreciated the use that could be made of it in criminal investigations. After looking through the unsolved crimes the department had on its books he became interested in the Lindörfer case. He asked Dr Lautenbach if he would continue to give assistance as he wished to reopen the investigation.

The forensic scientist readily agreed and Freund went off for his first visit to Reichelshofen. Friedrich Lindörfer met him at the door. This time the cooper smiled at the policeman and invited him in. Behaviour which puzzled the inspector, for in all the reports he'd read Lindörfer was described as a taciturn man not given to smiling at anyone.

But when the inspector went upstairs the reason became obvious. He soon came pounding down the stairs. 'Lindörfer! What have you been doing up in the attic?'

'Nothing,' said the man sullenly.

'Don't give me that! We took photographs of the attic as it used to be. Now it's all been changed. Quite a lot of objects which I see by my pictures used to be in certain positions are no longer there.'

'You must clear up in an attic, occasionally,' said the cooper slyly. 'Don't you do so in yours?'

'There was a pile of charcoal briquettes. What's happened to them?'

'We probably burnt those last winter.'

'And there was an old wooden bucket. What about that?'

The man merely shrugged his shoulders: 'I don't know. I've got work to do.' And he walked off.

The policeman was livid with frustration. But he was powerless to do anything. Lindörfer had a perfect right to dispose of any property which the police had not confiscated. The investigation had been mishandled from the start, he thought. The man had been allowed far too much time to destroy evidence and now there was almost none left. But Freund's frustration produced a determination to pursue this case and not to let go until a conclusion had been reached.

He went back up to the attic and began a meticulous examination of everything within it. Eventually he came across a pair of black women's shoes with faint brown stains on the insides and on the edges of the soles. He carefully wrapped these up and sent them off to Lautenbach.

The inspector visited the house three times in the following week, sending on to Lautenbach a cleaning rag which he found in the attic and the drain from the sink in case it still contained any traces of blood which might have been washed through it.

Soon after this he received a request to go and see the district attorney.

'I thought we'd decided that this case should be closed,' said that official, from the other side of his large desk. He didn't ask Freund to sit down.

'It seemed a good idea to reopen it,' said the inspector cheerfully.

'And have you found any evidence linking anyone at the house with the disappearance?' asked the district attorney, looking down at his nails.

'I found a pair of ladies' shoes in the attic which showed brown stains and Dr Lautenbach was able to show that the stains were definitely of blood and of group A, which we know is the same group as Lina Lindörfer.'

'It simply means, inspector, that she or any other person who has blood group A – and that applies to 40 per cent of the population – might have spilled some blood up there. And it doesn't mean she was murdered or, if she was, give us any indication who did it.'

'With respect, sir, Dr Lautenbach's results indicate that a considerable amount of blood was spilt in that attic—'

'Dr Lautenbach's results look pretty shaky to me,' interrupted the lawyer. 'And there's another thing. We're getting complaints from the villagers who feel that Lindörfer is being victimised. I tell you what I'll do.' He raised his hand as Freund opened his mouth to protest again. 'I'll give you another week to come up with enough evidence to arrest somebody. And if you haven't done so in that time, we'll have to finally close the case.'

'Very well, sir,' said the inspector, taking a deep breath. 'Will you get me another search warrant?'

On the 8th of May, Freund and Lautenbach appeared again at the house in Reichelshofen. Together they went up to the attic.

All around the gap where the piece of floorboard had been removed months ago they now found blood spatters. They also discovered stains on a cardboard carton which last year – according to the photographs – had stood near where the large bloodstain had been found. There were also signs of blood on an old coal box.

'We ought to construct a model of the room,' said Lautenbach. 'Then we could mark the position of every bloodstain we find. And if we look very carefully at each mark we might get an idea from its shape where it came from. I mean from which direction and with any luck from how far away. It will help us to reconstruct the crime.'

'Yes,' agreed Freund, 'and hopefully it will help to convince the district attorney that a murder has been committed here.'

While the scientist took his samples back to Erlangen, the inspector arranged for a wooden model of the attic to be built. Then the two of them took it, concealed in a large box, back to the farmhouse, where upstairs in the attic they carefuly copied each bloodstain on to its corresponding position on the model.

When they finished they had a picture of exactly where the crime had been committed. As they had suspected, the greatest concentration of blood was where the piece of floorboard had been removed. And it was quite obvious from the model that there had been a large outpouring of blood, indicating that major injuries had been inflicted on someone near the spot.

Dr Lautenbach quickly wrote a report on his findings and Freund rushed it, together with his own recommendations on the case and the model, to the district attorney's office. The policeman also asked for a warrant to arrest Lindörfer on a charge of murder.

He was quickly called in to see the official.

'You realise, Inspector Freund,' said the district attorney tapping the papers on the desk in front of him, 'that, interesting though all this is, it doesn't provide enough evidence to arrest a cat, never mind a human being?'

'We've got to do something,' protested the policeman. 'Every time I go he's destroyed more evidence. At this rate if we leave it much longer there won't be any left.'

'And you feel that if we arrest him, we'll be able to get him to confess?' He waited for Freund to reply and when the policeman didn't, he continued, 'I would remind you that this is 1963 and we are not the Gestapo. I know it's nearly twenty years since the war ended but people are still very sensitive about these things. I don't want there to be the slightest suspicion that the police are trying to beat a confession out of him.'

'I wasn't thinking of anything like that at all,' said Freund stiffly. 'I just feel that if we bring him in we might get some admissions from him.'

The district attorney sat for some time gazing into space and chewing the inside of his mouth. Eventually he spoke: 'All right. But you've got only a few hours to do it. Then we shall have to release him.'

Friedrich Lindörfer was arrested on the 22nd of June and the inspector began his interview. He took Lindörfer through his story time after time, pointing out where the cooper had changed his account. Then he asked him to explain the bloodstains found on the various articles. But he could not rattle Lindörfer. The stolid, taciturn countryman refused to change his story. Even when confronted with evidence he could not explain, like the bloodstained shoes, he merely shrugged his shoulders or answered simply, 'I don't know.'

The interviewing went on far into the night, then continued the next morning. The policeman was becoming exhausted, but the prisoner stubbornly continued his resistance.

During the evening of the second day Freund was accosted in the corridor outside the interview room by the district attorney.

'Any success?'

The policeman shook his head dolefully.

'You'll have to let him go tomorrow,' said the official, a smile of triumph lighting his face. 'And if you don't mind me saying so, inspector, I did warn you.' And with that he turned on his heel and walked away.

Freund continued his hunch-shouldered plodding way down the corridor. His legs felt like concrete, his back ached and his head felt as if it was filled with cotton wool. He had been going to get a cup of coffee, but suddenly he stopped.

Straightening his creaking back he returned to the interview room. 'Come with me,' he said to Lindörfer.

The sturdy countryman looked up at the policeman. He knew that Freund was as tired as he was. A slight smile crossed his face. 'You can't prove anything,' he croaked. Nevertheless he left the room.

They walked along the corridor and Freund opened a door. 'Inside,' he said. He didn't put on the light, but left the door open as he followed the man in. Light streamed in from the passage and he motioned Lindörfer to sit in a chair by the door. In the dim half-light the man did so. All he could see in front of him was the shape of a table.

Freund walked up to the table and looked back at Lindörfer. 'Bring your chair up.' He lifted his hand to the light pull.

When the light flooded down Lindörfer gasped. There on the table in front of him was the model.

'Do you recognise it? It's a faithful representation of your attic. Look, you can see where we've marked the bloodstains.' The man's eyes were standing out of his head. 'Can you see them? They pinpoint exactly the position where you struck your sister down.'

'No! It's not true!' The man buried his face in his hands.

'Yes, it is. You were finally going to have it out with her. You were angry and she was afraid of you. She locked her door, but you got some tools and broke it open. You chased her round the rooms and cornered her in the attic. There you felled her.'

'No! I didn't! It wasn't like that at all. It was an accident! I only wanted to talk to her, but she kept abusing me. She was ironing at the time. And then she struck me. I hit her back. Then I realised I was holding the iron. She staggered into the attic and fell by the pile of briquettes. When I realised she was dead, I was panic-stricken and didn't know what to do.'

He then went on to describe how he had dragged the body downstairs in an old coat and hidden it under straw in the pigsty. Later he gave details of the dismemberment of the corpse; his attempts to burn it in the workshop stove and the eventual boiling of the remains in the large kettle he used for cleaning cider barrels. And he took the police to the places where he spread the bones and the remaining flesh.

He also described the weeks of painstaking scrubbing and cleaning to remove what he hoped would be the last vestiges of his crime, and the repainting of the stairs and other places where he was not sure that washing would be enough.

But however hard he had tried he had not been able to remove those last traces which Dr Lautenbach had been able to find and which were to bring home the crime to him.

He was convicted at the court in Ansbach of man-slaughter and was sentenced to eight years in prison.

3

Buried Down Under

'Albert,' she said. 'You've not been straight with me.'

The couple were walking up an overgrown path from the street to the villa. The man glanced at his companion nervously. He was thickset, fair-haired and wearing the characteristic sidewhiskers of the 1890s. He was about forty, whereas she could not have been much more than twenty.

'My dear Emily, whatever can you mean? Here am I going out of my way to do you a kindness by showing you round the house and you reward me with accusations of not being straightforward.'

Emily had screwed up her courage to the point where she could confront him, but for the moment it deserted her. 'I thought we were . . . well, walking out,' she muttered.

'Of course we are. Of course we are, but—'

'No, Albert.' She took a deep breath and stopped him with a hand on his arm, as if she was afraid that he would overwhelm her with words, as he had so often in the past. They stood in the middle of the path with Emily gazing earnestly at Albert. 'Tell me the truth. Were you with another woman the other night in the bar of the Commercial Hotel?'

He stepped back in surprise, a blank look on his face.

'Well, as you know,' he began slowly, 'I live at the Commercial Hotel . . . ' Then a slow smile twitched the corners of his lips. 'Well now, Emily Mather, and what if I were to admit it?'

She immediately flushed scarlet and tears sprang into her eyes. For a moment an undecided look appeared on her face, then her chin went up. She was about to swing round and depart without another word when Albert caught her arm.

'Emily! Emily! Don't jump to conclusions. I freely admit that I was with another woman. But she's my sister!'

The girl turned to look at him. 'Your sister?'

'Certainly. She lives in Liverpool – well Birkenhead – with her husband and four children. He went off to California and she was to join him there. They had to give up their house and since Birkenhead is only a few miles from here I offered her accommodation until her ship sailed from Plymouth. In fact she was occupying this very house until a few days ago.'

'Albert, are you telling me the truth?'

The stocky man drew himself up. 'If you don't believe what I'm saying, Emily, the remedy is in your own hands. Just go back.' And with that he turned and continued alone up the path towards the house.

The young girl, after standing irresolute for a moment, rushed after him. 'Albert! Don't be angry.'

He stopped and allowed her to catch him up. And with the abrupt change of mood that was so characteristic of the man he crooked his arm, so that she could take it, and smiled down at her.

She took it gingerly and looked up at him shyly. 'I believe you, Albert,' she said softly.

'Good,' he said in a matter-of-fact voice. 'Now, as I was telling you, this is the villa I've rented for my good friend Colonel Brooks.' They continued up to the house. There he produced a key and opened the front door.

'When did you say you expected him to move in?'

'I don't know. He's at the War Office in London at the moment and he asked me to have some work done on the floors before he arrived. Very fussy is the colonel.'

They began their tour of the house. But Emily was more intrigued with the question of army ranks. 'Albert, is a colonel higher than inspector of regiments?'

'My rank, you mean? No, inspector of regiments is not really a rank at all, it's a civilian appointment.'

'But I've seen you in your uniform.'

'Oh yes, but that's just for ceremonies. I'm a civilian really. But I must tell you, my dear Emily, that the army and I are about to part company.' He looked around as if in that empty house he expected someone could hear him. Then he walked ahead of the girl into the kitchen. 'What do you think of the floor here? I've just had it relaid to suit the colonel.'

'Yes, very nice, Albert. But what did you mean about parting company with the army?' She looked at him uneasily.

'Well it means that I am soon going to leave this fine little town and journey to the wilds of South Africa. I'm a mining engineer, really. This is what I was trained for and I've only been helping the army out with advice on what regiments need for tunnelling and suchlike. But I've been offered a job at £2,000 a year to be manager of a gold mine near Johannesburg. What do you think of that?'

'Leave Rainhill?'

'I shall have to, shan't I? There aren't many gold mines around here.' And he laughed uproariously.

'I didn't know you'd be going . . . quite so soon.'

'Yes, I'm sorry, my dear, to spring it on you like this, but I only learnt about it myself the other day. I've been here nearly two months, which is a long time for anyone connected with the army to be in any particular place. I've already booked my farewell dinner at the Commercial Hotel. I've invited all the friends I've met here. It'll be a good night.'

'I'm sure it will,' said Emily in a low voice. 'But . . . but what about us?'

'Ah yes. That does raise a problem. I couldn't possibly ask you to accompany me all the way to South Africa.' Here his voice dropped. 'Unless it was as my wife.'

'What?'

He slipped an arm round her waist. 'Emily Mather, I'm asking you to marry me.'

The girl backed away. 'Keep your hands to yourself, Albert Williams!'

'Don't you want to marry me?'

'I didn't say that.'

'Well then, while you're thinking about it, why don't we dance?' He followed as she backed away until she was up against the wall and couldn't move any further. Slipping his right arm round her waist and grasping her left hand in his he whirled her round in a waltz on the new concrete floor.

'Oh, Albert. You are a one!'

About six months after this incident, on Thursday, 3 March 1892, the owner of an empty house in Andrews Street, Windsor, a suburb of Melbourne, Australia, was taking a prospective client round the property. Although it was the end of the Australian summer it was still very hot that day and the client had taken off her hat and was fanning herself with it.

'It's a nice house,' she said, 'but you'll certainly have to do something about those drains.'

The owner pretended that he hadn't noticed the smell until then. 'I can assure you that the drains were thoroughly cleaned out not long ago. Now you mention it, there may be a slight smell, but I thought it was coming from outside, possibly from next door.'

'No, it's definitely from inside. It's strongest in one of the bedrooms.'

Later the owner contacted the agent. 'Did you know there's an awful smell coming from one of the bedrooms? We've just lost a sale because of it.'

The agent promised to come and look round the property and later that day the two men went into the offending bedroom.

'It may be something in the chimney,' said the agent. 'A bird or a cat, perhaps, got stuck and died and the hot weather is causing it to smell. I'll get a crowbar and see if we can dislodge anything.'

But they found nothing in the chimney and, since both of them were now feeling sick, they went to the window to breathe some fresh air. After a while the owner turned to look back at the fireplace.

'Look at that hearth,' he said. 'Somebody's replaced the hearth stone with concrete.'

'Not a very good job they've made of it either,' remarked the agent. 'It doesn't fit very well and the heat has caused the concrete to crack.'

He walked towards it and, using his crowbar, was easily able to lever up part of the hearth. Then he dropped the iron bar and his face went green. He staggered away, one hand clutching his throat as if he was choking, the other pointing down into the hole he had just made. He was sick in the corner of the room.

The police were called and eventually Detective Sergeant William Considine, of the Melbourne CID, and his assistant, Detective Henry Cawsey, appeared on the scene. The hole in the hearth was widened by policemen working with wet handkerchiefs tied over their faces and soon the cause of the smell was revealed – the decomposing body of a young woman in her nightdress. Her head had been battered and her throat cut. And she appeared to have been there several weeks.

When the body had been removed to the mortuary for a postmortem and the windows opened to disperse the smell Detective Cawsey began a painstaking search of the premises while Considine went to interview the house agent.

That individual told him that the last tenant had been a man called Druin. He and his wife had moved in on the 16th of December and paid a month's rent in advance. But they moved out within a few days without contacting him.

'Can you give me a description of them?'

The estate agent remembered them only vaguely. 'I can tell you this though. The man came from the Old Country. I recognised that from his accent. And I don't think they'd been here very long.'

The detective next talked to the neighbours in Andrews Street. One of them was able to give a good description of the couple and in addition spoke of a commotion at the Druin house just before Christmas.

'There was shouting and carrying on late into the night. I told my husband if it didn't stop soon he would have to call the police. This is a respectable neighbourhood. We can't have goings on like that!'

'Yes, yes,' said the detective. 'Did you call the police?'

'Well, no, we didn't in the end. But I saw her the next afternoon in the back garden hanging out some clothes. She looked awful. She had a black eye and bruises on her face. But when I called out to her she scuttled back inside without answering.'

When Considine returned to detective headquarters he talked to his assistant, Cawsey. 'From the descriptions I've managed to obtain,' he said, 'I think we can safely say that the dead woman is Mrs Druin.' He went on to tell the other detective of his talk with the estate agent.

'That's very interesting,' said the assistant. 'In the rubbish in one of the rooms I found a torn luggage receipt from the steamship *Kaiser Wilhelm II*, which came from England and docked in Melbourne on the 9th of December.'

'Yes, that would fit.'

'And there's something else.' He put a crumpled and torn card on the desk.

The detective sergeant smoothed it out and turned the card over. It was a little smaller than a postcard. 'It's an invitation,' he said. Then reading from the pasteboard: ' "Mr Albert Williams requests the pleasure of the company of . . . " there's a gap, then it goes on: "at dinner at the Commercial Hotel, Rainhill." '

'Where's Rainhill?' asked Cawsey.

Considine shook his head. 'Get hold of an atlas and we'll look it up.'

Some time later they established that Rainhill was a small town near Liverpool.

'Do you think this has anything to do with Druin?' asked Detective Cawsey.

'These cards,' replied Considine, 'are what you send out yourself. Since there's no name in the space it follows that it belonged to Albert Williams. Of course we've no proof, but my guess is that Albert Williams is Druin. We'll proceed on that basis for the moment anyway. I'll get off a cable to Scotland Yard and ask them to look out for him in case he's gone back to England.'

Considine and Cawsey then traced as many of the passengers of the *Kaiser Wilhelm II* as they could. Quite a few remembered Williams. Although accompanied by his wife, he had quickly gained a reputation for flirting with all the pretty women on board. He was a boisterous character who wore a lot of jewellery and was regarded with some suspicion by many passengers when he tried to interest them in various money-making schemes.

'He said he was a mining engineer,' said one. 'And originally he'd been going to South Africa, but had then accepted a better-paid job in Australia. But I didn't believe him. He was nothing but a con-man.'

A few days later Detective Cawsey had some news for his boss. 'I think I've got some more on this Druin or Williams,' he said. 'A man of the same description bought some cement and a spade from a builder near Andrews Street. But he used the name Dobson.'

'Dobson,' said Considine reflectively. 'That name rings a bell.' He got up and began rummaging in a cabinet, coming up with a number of files which he dumped on the desk in front of him. After sorting through them for some time he picked out one and sat down at the desk with it. 'Here's the one, I'm sure.' He began to read. 'Yes, this is it. A man of Druin's description, using the name Dobson, managed to swindle Kilpatrick and Co – you know, the jewellery firm – out of some very valuable items. And this was' – he turned back to the first page – 'just before the New Year.'

A few weeks before these events took place a pretty eighteen-year-old called Kate Rounsefell was travelling on a coastal steamer from the south coast town of Adelaide to the east coast town of Sydney. In those days sea travel between coastal towns in Australia was the preferred mode of transport, since the roads were largely non-existent and the trains were cramped and very hot in summer.

The coaster put in to Melbourne to unload and take on some passengers. Although it carried few travellers, Kate took little notice of the thickset, fair-haired man who came aboard there. But later, when they all sat down to dinner together round the large table in the lounge, he managed to sit next to her and soon engaged her in conversation.

She told him that she was going to Bathurst, a small town a hundred miles up country from Sydney, to stay with her sister.

Kate was intrigued by the rather flashy-looking stranger, by his accent and by his name and title. He announced himself as Baron Swanston.

The journey from Melbourne to Sydney took only two days, but in that time Swanston monopolised Kate. He was amusing and attentive, and his man-of-the-world confidence fascinated her. He told her that he was a mining engineer, and seemed to have a fund of stories from South Africa, South America and Great

Britain, and he said that as a young man he had lived in Australia.

The ship docked in Sydney at about midday on the 14th of January. The baron found a cab and supervised the loading of their luggage into it.

'I'll take you to the station, Miss Rounsefell,' he said, 'then I'll carry on to my hotel.'

But at the station he had bad news for her. 'I'm afraid you've just missed the last train to Bathurst today.'

Kate's face expressed concern.

'I don't want to influence you in any way,' continued the baron, 'but as it looks as if you may be considering staying in Sydney overnight, I might mention that I shall be stopping at the Wentworth Hotel. It's not too ostentatious, but is comfortable and I can recommend it unreservedly.'

'Why, thank you, Baron. I shall be pleased to accept your suggestion.'

'Please call me Frederick . . . Kate.'

Swanston booked rooms for them in the hotel, then took the young girl on a tour of the city. Later that evening over a candlelit dinner, which included a bottle of expensive imported wine, he reached across the table and took her hand.

'Kate, will you marry me?'

She withdrew her hand immediately: 'Frederick! We've only known each other two days!'

'Ah yes, but love blossoms very quickly.'

Kate was undoubtedly attracted by the baron. The intense interest of the older and more experienced man in the innocent eighteen-year-old drew her like a magnet. He appeared to be quite wealthy, to have prospects of a good job and a secure future. On the other hand she knew nothing definite about him. She went to bed that night with her head in a whirl.

The next day they met at breakfast. The baron said nothing further about his proposal of the night before, but smiled at her across the table. 'I hope you won't think me presumptuous, Kate, but as it's such a lovely day, if you aren't desperate to catch the early train, I could show you Coogee beach.'

A few hours later they walked across the sunlit beach and listened to the waves crashing on the shore. Frederick took her hand in his again.

'Kate,' he said. 'Do you remember what I asked you last night?'

This time she left her hand in his for a little longer before she withdrew it.

'Don't keep me in suspense, Kate.'

The young girl cleared her throat. 'I don't know, Frederick. We've known each other such a short while . . . ' She was not finding it easy to speak. 'If . . . if you could find the time to come and see me while I'm at my sister's house . . . '

'Of course I will, my dear. When I've finished my business in Sydney I'll come.'

A few days later the baron arrived and over dinner the first night imparted his good news.

'I've just been offered the job of mine manager at a gold mine in Southern Cross.'

'Where on earth's that?' enquired Kate's sister.

'In Western Australia,' replied Frederick, 'a couple of hundred miles inland from Perth.'

'That would mean Kate living at the back of beyond?'

'Certainly not. Southern Cross is a thriving small town and of course as mine manager I would have my own house.'

But Kate's sister pressed him for details of the firm he was to work for and for more information about himself and his background.

The next day Frederick took the young girl for a buggy ride. They drove out of town and the baron reined in the horse under some shady trees just off the road.

He turned to her. 'Your sister doesn't seem to like me.'

'Oh she does, really. It's just that being older, she tries to look after me and tends to be very suspicious of any gentlemen friends I may have.'

'Kate.' Frederick fumbled in his pocket and brought out a silver cameo pendant on a thin chain. 'I want you to have this. It's quite valuable I believe, but that's not the point. It's very precious to me because it belonged to my mother. Even if I never see you again I want to think of you wearing it.'

Tears welled in Kate's eyes. 'Why, it's beautiful, Frederick.'

When they returned to the house the young girl's eyes were shining and she was wearing the pendant. 'We're going to be married!' she cried. 'Frederick's going to Southern Cross first and he will make all the arrangements there. Then I will follow when he sends for me.'

When the baron finally left for Sydney, where he was to board the *Oceana* for Fremantle in Western Australia, Kate's sister drew her aside.

'I think you're making a mistake. He's much older than you and there's something about him . . . I don't know . . . It sends cold shivers down my spine.'

The young girl laughed: 'You're exaggerating. He's a decent, lovable man. And I'm going to marry him.'

'There's one thing about it,' said the sister grimly. 'I bet you never hear from him again.'

But she was wrong. There followed an avalanche of letters and telegrams, all expressing Frederick's undying love and affection. After several weeks came the expected wire. 'Come at once,' it said and with it came £20 to pay Kate's fare and expenses.

She had been packed up ready for days and she set off without delay by train for Melbourne, where she would stay in a hotel – already booked for her by a relative – until she embarked for Western Australia.

In the detective headquarters in Melbourne things were moving swiftly. Detective Sergeant Considine was reading a report when he suddenly yelled for his assistant. When Detective Cawsey appeared, Considine threw the report across the desk to him.

'Read that! No, don't bother, I'll tell you what's in it!'

Cawsey took a chair and sat down opposite his boss. He had rarely seen the man so disturbed. Considine's face was flushed and his eyes were bulging in an angry manner.

'Do you realise we've got a mass murderer on our hands?' He banged on the report in front of him. 'This is from the Lancashire Police in England. Our Druin, Dobson or Albert Williams is actually one Frederick Bayley Deeming. He comes from somewhere near Liverpool, where he has two brothers. Following up our enquiry, passed on from Scotland Yard, they found he'd been parading around a town called Rainhill as an inspector of regiments, which he wasn't, and wearing a uniform he'd hired from a theatrical costumier in London! He'd also rented a villa for a Colonel Brooks – who doesn't exist!'

'What about his wife?' asked Cawsey.

'Which one?' screeched Considine. 'When the Lancashire police learned of our suspicions about Deeming burying his wife in the house in Andrews Street, they started to put two and two together. Someone remembered that there was an entirely new floor put in the kitchen in this villa he'd taken. They dug up the kitchen floor. And what do you think they found?'

'I shudder to think.'

'You're right. Under the concrete were five bodies! A woman and four young children. All had their throats cut except one, a nine-year-old girl, who had been strangled! I tell you we're dealing with a monster!'

'Who were they?' enquired Cawsey hurriedly, in an effort to calm his boss.

'They were identified by Deeming's two brothers from Birkenhead, who came forward when the find was reported in the paper. The bodies were Deeming's wife Marie, a Welsh girl he married in' – here he turned over some pages – '1881, that's over ten years ago, and their four children.

'He also has a record of imprisonment.' He consulted the document in front of him again. 'Just before this business in Rainhill he'd been serving a sentence for defrauding some jewellers in Hull. In 1883 he came to Australia and set up as a gas-fitter in Sydney, but was imprisoned for theft. Later he went bankrupt and was jailed for fraud. He left for South Africa in 1887. There he acquired a pretty unsavoury reputation in the gold fields at Johannesburg for selling worthless mines. And there were a couple of women, associated with him there, who disappeared in suspicious circumstances. I tell you this man is a fiend!'

'Have we got any information on the second Mrs Deeming?' enquired Cawsey. 'The one he buried in the house in Andrews Street?'

'Yes, she was an Emily Mather, the daughter of a shopkeeper in Rainhill. He courted her while he was in the town even though his wife and four children were not far away in Birkenhead. Then he invited his wife and family to stay at the villa – neighbours remember seeing them there for a few days – and quite deliberately slaughtered them and buried their bodies under the kitchen floor. But what's important as far as we're concerned is that he's liable to do it again.'

'You think so?'

'He kills his first wife last year just to clear the way for him to marry this Emily Mather. He didn't make any money out of it, as far as I can see. Then, within a few months, he's got rid of Emily in the same way. Who's he got rid of her for?'

'I see what you mean.'

'I think we're going to have to give it to the newspapers. If we get them to publish a good description of him, together with some of his aliases, somebody is sure to recognise it.'

'Yes, but he might see it himself,' argued Cawsey. 'And if he does, he's only got to bury himself in one of those remote mining camps or simply disappear into the bush and we'll never find him.'

'We'll have to risk it, if only to protect any women who might be taken in by him. Otherwise there's going to be another murder, of that I'm sure.'

'If it's not already happened,' muttered Cawsey. 'Do you think,' he continued slowly, 'that it's possible he's this Jack the Ripper they have in London?'

The newspaper story brought immediate results. An observant shipping clerk recognised that the description fitted a certain Baron Swanston who had booked a passage from Melbourne to Sydney several weeks before. He went to the police who began an immediate search for the baron in Sydney.

At about the same time Kate's sister also recognised the description and she communicated with the police. They showed her a picture of Deeming and she recognised him at once as Baron Swanston. But the young girl had already left to join Deeming.

Hurriedly Kate's sister telegraphed the hotel in Melbourne, the Federal Coffee Palace, where Kate was to have spent the night before catching a ship to Western Australia. The telegram read: 'For God's sake go no further.'

The police, having received details of where Deeming was from Kate's sister, wired the Perth police and asked them to look for him at Southern Cross.

Kate Rounsefell, unsure what to do after receiving her sister's telegram, sent back a message asking for more details. She went out for a walk that evening in Melbourne to try and calm her troubled thoughts. When she saw the latest edition of a newspaper on sale she bought a copy. It carried the banner headline: 'Windsor Murderer Arrested'.

Inside appeared details of how Frederick Deeming, alias Baron Swanston, had been picked up at the mining camp.

Detective Cawsey made the long journey to Western Australia with extradition papers, since Deeming had been arrested in a different state to the one where the crime was committed. After a hearing before a magistrate in Perth, during which Deeming's solicitor made strenuous efforts to delay the proceedings, the prisoner was transferred to Cawsey's custody for the trip back to Melbourne.

On the return journey, by train from Perth to Albany to pick up a ship to take them to Melbourne, the prisoner was besieged at nearly every station by angry mobs who would have lynched him had there not been a strong police presence to protect him.

At his trial a parade of witnesses were able to provide a strong case against Deeming – albeit a circumstantial one – for the murder of Emily Mather. His defence was insanity, but there was very little evidence to support this. He complained from the dock, before the jury retired, that he had not had a fair trial and that he had been tried and found guilty by the press – which was perfectly true. Nevertheless he was undoubtedly guilty of Emily Mather's murder and the jury brought in a verdict to that effect, also stating that they did not think he was insane. On 23 May 1892, he was hanged in Melbourne Jail.

There is very little evidence to support Deeming's alleged claim to his solicitor that he was the perpetrator of the last two of the Jack the Ripper murders in Whitechapel, although at least some of the Melbourne police believed it was true.

4

Mind Over Matter

The Model T Ford chugged its way up the hill and stopped outside the small wooden farmhouse at the top. The house, which was set back forty feet from the road, overlooked the Vermilion River valley, eighty miles east of Edmonton in Canada. It was about 6.30 on a warm evening in July 1928.

In the front garden was a young man in his early twenties with dark straight hair, a clean-cut face and the lithe body of an athlete. He looked up as the car stopped in the road and a portly figure alighted.

'Is your brother at home, Vernon?' asked the driver in a peremptory voice.

The young man shook his head. 'Fred's in the fields, Councillor Scott.'

The other man nodded his head. He was always pleased when people used his title. 'I've brought a tax receipt for him.' He waved a slip of paper in the air. 'Will you pass it on?'

Vernon approached the local councillor. 'Sure.' He held out his hand.

But Scott did not immediately hand it over. 'You will be sure to give it to him?'

He was thinking, not for the first time, what a contrast there was between the two Booher brothers. Fred, only twenty-four, was turning out to be a model farmer. Hardworking and industrious, he had already bought the farm on which the two men were now standing. Vernon, on the other hand, who was four years younger, seemed to have little interest in farming and spent most of his time playing hockey.

Young Vernon's face flushed when he saw the councillor's hesitation. 'Of course I will,' he snapped and, almost snatching the piece of paper from Scott's hand, turned his back and walked in the direction of the house.

The councillor was at once contrite and tried to mollify the young man. 'How's the hockey going?' he hurriedly asked the retreating back.

Vernon Booher turned round immediately and his face was alive with interest. 'Very good,' he said. 'Last month I came back from two weeks' touring with the local team and there's a possibility that I may get a trial with the provinces.'

The councillor allowed himself a sly smile. 'How's your mother feel about it, Vernon?'

The young man's face fell. Scott didn't need an answer. He knew very well that although Eunice Booher kept house for the two brothers, coming over every day from the home farm, four miles to the north, that she shared with her husband and two younger daughters, Fred was her favourite. In fact there were even rumours that Mrs Booher was opposing the relationship between Vernon and a young nurse.

Before the young man could reply he noticed that Scott was looking back down the hill. Booher turned and saw another young man coming up from the direction of the fields.

The second man looked up and waved at the two by the garden gate then turned towards the small house.

Vernon's face suddenly contorted. 'Don't go in there!' he yelled.

The man from the fields pulled up short.

'Go into the barn, Bill, and feed the pigs.' Vernon's voice was now more moderated. But as the young man turned away to do as he was told, Councillor Scott gave Vernon Booher a curious look.

It was around ten o'clock that night, just as it was getting dark, that Vernon Booher burst into the farmhouse next to his, which belonged to Robert Ross. The young man was obviously very emotional and overwrought. 'Bob!' he shouted. 'Ma and Fred have been shot!'

Ross gripped Vernon's arm. 'Calm down,' he said, 'and I'll telephone for Dr Heaslip.'

The doctor arrived a little later outside the Booher farmhouse in his car. There was still some light in the night sky and from this he could see the house. The one-storey building stood dark against the paler sky. There was a lean-to on the left-hand side of the house which contained the kitchen. And further over to the left stood a barn. Off to the right was the bunkhouse, which was little more than the size of a small horse-box and was on wheels. There appeared to be no one about.

Then Dr Heaslip heard the sound of voices and out

of the gloom, from the direction of the fields, came
Vernon Booher leading two horses on which were sitting his teenaged sisters Dorothy and Algirtha. The
two girls were crying.

The young man saw the doctor standing by the gate
and, leaving the horses, came forward to meet him.

'Have you been inside?' he asked. The doctor shook
his head. 'They're all dead in there,' continued Vernon,
his voice quite calm. He turned to his sisters. 'You two
stay out here.' Then he led the way into the house
through the kitchen door.

He stepped over something just inside the door:
'Wait there a minute, Doctor, I'll get a light.' A
moment later he appeared with an oil lamp.

Dr Heaslip could then see that there was a body on
the floor just inside the kitchen door. He bent to examine it.

'It's Fred,' reported the doctor. 'I'm afraid he's quite
dead. Looks as if he's been shot through the mouth.
But he's still got his hat on. Perhaps he was shot on
his way out.'

'Or on his way in,' came the dry voice of the young
man.

The doctor stepped over the body and followed
Vernon into the next room, only a few feet away. This
was a small dining room. There, under the fitful light
of the oil lamp, a dreadful sight met his eyes.

Partially sitting in a chair, but tilted forward so that
were it not for the table interposing she would have
tumbled on to the floor, was the figure of a middle-

aged woman. The back of her head had been blown away.

An exclamation of horror was wrenched from the doctor's lips as he bent to examine the corpse. 'It's your mother, Vernon.'

The young man said nothing.

'My God! This is awful,' cried the doctor.

'I'm afraid it's not the end, Doctor,' came the quiet voice of the young man. 'Gabriel's dead in the bunkhouse.'

He led the way to the bunkhouse. It was a narrow room having space for little more than two bunk beds. There, slumped between the beds and the wall, lay the body of Gabriel Goromby, one of the hired hands. He was lying on his back and had been shot, once through the breast and twice through the head.

'Sheer slaughter,' muttered the doctor as he bent to examine the third victim. Then he looked up at Vernon, who was standing outside looking in. 'Whoever could have done it?'

The young man shrugged his shoulders. 'I don't know. There were a couple of Hungarians around here yesterday. Gabriel is a Hungarian, you know. And they seemed to want him to go away with them. I didn't hear all of it. They were arguing with Fred. But I gather that he wouldn't let Gabriel go with them.'

The doctor climbed to his feet and stumbled outside into the cool evening air. When he had taken a few deep breaths he turned to Booher.

'Don't you have another hired hand?'

'Yes,' said the young man slowly. 'There's a Polish

boy called Bill. I suppose he could be responsible, I haven't seem him around tonight.'

Dorothy Booher appeared out of the gloom. She had obviously heard her brother's words. 'Bill's a nice boy,' she said stoutly. 'He wouldn't do a dreadful thing like this.'

'Well, we shall have to report the matter to the police as soon as we can,' said the doctor. 'I'm afraid there's nothing I can do for any of them.'

Vernon, the two girls and the doctor all piled into the medical man's car and drove to the Ross place to phone.

Constable Olsen of the Alberta Provincial Police, stationed in the nearest town to the Booher farm, Mannville, arrived about an hour later. After a brief examination of the bodies by the light of lanterns he ordered everybody out of the buildings and into the back yard for questioning. By this time Henry Booher, the father of the family, had arrived. He explained that he had been working in the fields some way to the north and had heard no gun shots.

'Is there anything missing?' asked the constable.

Henry Booher shook his head. 'Not as far as I know.'

Vernon Booher confirmed this and repeated to the constable the incident of the strange men at the farm the previous day. 'I did hear the shots,' he continued. 'It must have been about eight o'clock or a little earlier. I was fetching the cows in and the shots seemed to come from the direction of the house. I rushed back and found Fred and Ma and Gabriel, but I didn't see anybody else.'

'Well, it's a bit late to make a search for Bill tonight,' said the constable. 'We'll start in the morning at first light.'

'I don't think anybody's looked in the barn yet,' said Henry Booher.

With a lantern in his hand Olsen swung open the barn door and entered, closely followed by Vernon and his father. There in the middle aisle, between the pig pens, lay the body of Bill. He was lying on his back with a bucket not far from his outstretched right hand. He had been shot, once in the face and once in the abdomen. And he was dead.

There was little more that the constable could do that night, so after securing the doors of the farmhouse, bunkhouse and barn, he went back to report to his superiors by phone.

At first light he was back again and carefully examined the buildings and the ground between them. He found a .22 rifle and an old shotgun in the house, but they had obviously not been fired for months. But he found no rifle shells. All the murdered people looked to have been killed by rifle bullets, but the murderer must have afterwards picked up all the ejected cartridge cases. A remarkably cool customer, surmised the constable.

In the afternoon he was joined by Detective Sergeant Leslie from the headquarters of the Alberta Provincial Police in Edmonton.

'Do you want to interview witnesses?' asked Olsen indicating the group of onlookers who were hanging around near the farmhouse.

The sergeant shook his head. 'Let's have a look around first.'

The constable took his superior officer into the farmhouse and showed him the carnage within. He explained about the lack of rifle shells.

Leslie nodded and surveyed the scene. 'Let's see, now. Mrs Booher was sitting at the table in the dining room. She was apparently picking the stalks and leaves from a bowl of strawberries, with her back to the door which leads to the kitchen. Somebody shot her in the back of the head, possibly from the doorway, here, or from a little further back in the kitchen. Then Fred Booher rushes in, having heard the shots. The killer turns and fires at Fred, who takes a bullet through the mouth and falls to the floor, there. And while he's lying on the floor he gets another round through the head to finish him off. But all the time the murderer ought to be ejecting the cases from the rifle.'

The detective had positioned himself where the murderer must have stood, just in front of the stove. Now he looked around carefully and spied a saucepan with water in it, behind him on the kitchen stove.

Leslie looked into the pan, then cried, 'And here is one!' He dipped his hand in and came up with an ejected cartridge case. He held out the dripping brass tube to the constable. 'What do you think? .303?'

Olsen, whose eyes had bulged with surprise, could only nod dumbly.

'What must have happened', continued the detective imperturbably, 'was that when he worked the bolt one of the cases spun up over his shoulder and plopped unnoticed into the pan of water behind him.'

The bodies were removed to the mortuary in Mannville later that afternoon and the policemen began the task of interviewing people around the farm.

Because Vernon Booher was a material witness he was held in custody in the fire-station in Mannville. Meanwhile, a few days later, Leslie returned to report to his chief in Edmonton.

'There's little doubt in my mind', he said, 'that Vernon Booher is the murderer.' The sergeant was sitting in Police Chief Mike Gier's office at police headquarters.

Gier raised his eyebrows. 'Remind me of the details,' he said.

'Well, Robert Ross, who has a farm next to the Boohers, saw Fred Booher on his way towards the Booher house on the evening of the murder at about six o'clock. In fact they stopped and spoke. Fred said he was going to relieve the hired hand Goromby who was working on a tractor in a nearby field. And to do this he would have had to pass very close to the farmhouse. A few minutes after this Ross heard shots coming from the direction of the Booher house.'

'Did he go and investigate?' enquired the police chief.

Leslie shook his head: 'It's not uncommon to hear shots in that area. There's a fair amount of rabbit shooting goes on there.'

'Go on with your story.'

'As I say, this was about six o'clock, or a little after. About the same time the two Booher girls, who were on their way into town on horseback to go to the pictures and not far from the Booher house, also heard shots coming from that direction.'

'All right, we'll say that Fred and Mrs Booher were shot at six. What about it?'

'Well, sir, about half past six Councillor Scott came to the house to deliver a tax receipt and saw Vernon in the garden. Then the hired man Bill arrived. By the way his real name was Wasyl Rosiuk, and he was a Polack. Well, anyway, when it looked as if he was going to go into the house Vernon Booher ordered him away and told him to go and feed the pigs in the barn. Which, incidentally, was where he was found, shot dead, with his feeding pail nearby.'

'So you think Booher shot his mother and brother at six and then went after this Rosiuk and shot him after Councillor Scott had left?'

'That's about it. There were some more shots heard by Ross at about eight o'clock, again from the direction of the Booher house, and they were also heard by his wife. I think that was when Goromby came back, having got tired of waiting to be relieved. He must have gone to the bunkhouse and was killed there by Vernon, who was waiting for him to come home.'

'Sounds as if this Booher is a cold, calculating character.'

'I think he is. And he's none too popular in the area at the moment either. They're a strongly religious community and the dead people were all well liked.'

The police chief nodded. 'What's his story?'

'He claims to have heard shots only at eight and to

have rushed home then and found his brother, mother and Goromby dead.'

'Have you any evidence he didn't?'

'No, sir, but if he did what he says, why didn't he hear the shots at six? He was near enough at half past to see Councillor Scott.'

Mike Gier pursed his lips. 'It's an interesting theory. Have you some proof? What about the rifle? Have you found that?'

Leslie could only shake his head. 'There appears to be only one .303 rifle in that area. It's owned by an old timer called Charles Stephenson who's a neighbour of the Boohers. He actually loaned the rifle to Fred last fall. But it was returned and used to hang behind the kitchen door. But strangely enough it's been missing since last Sunday – the day before the murder. The Stephenson family all go to church on a Sunday and the house is left empty and unlocked. It could easily have been taken then – stolen by Vernon Booher.'

'You can prove that?'

'Every week, someone from the Booher family is detailed to go to the Austin place. It's an unoccupied farm which they rent, not very far from Stephenson's place. Someone has to ride up there and check on the fences. Last Sunday Vernon volunteered to go and was later seen by several people in the vicinity of the Stephenson farm.'

'It's all suspicion,' mused the police chief. 'We've no proof. You've searched for the gun around the Booher house?'

'I've had twenty men scouring the place and the fields around. We haven't found a thing.'

Mike Gier sat for a long time in silence. He seemed to be gazing at the ceiling. Then he asked, 'Have you ever heard of a Dr Maximilian Langsner?'

Leslie frowned for a moment, then his face lightened. 'Isn't he some sort of stage hypnotist?'

The police chief cleared his throat. 'He's been . . . quite useful to the authorities on a number of occasions.'

The sergeant said nothing.

His boss continued, 'There was a case in Vancouver where the police picked up a suspect in a jewellery robbery, but they couldn't find the loot. Dr Langsner said he might be able to help and was placed in the suspect's cell. He stayed there for half an hour and said not a word to the man. Then he came out and reported that the police would find the jewels in a room with yellow walls, hidden behind a picture. They were a bit puzzled by this as the fellow's flat didn't have a yellow wall in it. But when they searched his girlfriend's apartment, in a room with yellow wallpaper they found the jewels, just as Dr Langsner had said, behind a picture.'

'What's that supposed to show,' scoffed the sergeant, 'that he read the suspect's mind?'

'It's easy to laugh. But we don't know what he might be capable of. And if he can help you to find that rifle, well, can you afford to turn down any assistance?'

The vague suspicion which had been forming in Leslie's mind grew to a certainty. 'You've been in touch with him then, sir?'

Gier nodded his head. 'He's arriving on the noon train.'

Detective Sergeant Jim Leslie stood on the platform at Edmonton station feeling highly disgruntled with the whole business, not least because he had been detailed to meet the doctor. Nevertheless he had prepared a little speech of welcome and when the small untidy-looking figure alighted from the train he stepped forward, introduced himself and made his speech.

'Welcome to Edmonton. We are very happy you could come and I hope we'll be able to work together successfully.'

There was a twinkle in the little man's eyes as he replied in a rather high voice, 'I don't believe a word of it. You are not at all pleased to see me. But all the same I hope I shall be able to help and that we shall become friends.'

Back in the chief of police's office the little doctor with the long unruly hair gave some account of himself: 'I was born in Vienna in 1893 and attended the Universities of Vienna, Leipzig and Graz, receiving the degree of bachelor of arts from Graz. Then I studied anatomy and philosophy in the Scandinavian countries before doing research in experimental psychology at the University of Uppsala in Sweden. I then travelled the world spending some time in India where I obtained my doctorate. It was there that I was introduced to the intuitive control of the mind and much of my power stems from this.'

'What brings you to Canada?' asked Leslie, who was

becoming impressed with the little man in spite of himself.

'I want to study the Eskimos,' piped Langsner. 'So many primitive peoples have become corrupted by Western influences, but not the Eskimos. They can sense weather changes and even danger long before it comes. I want to go and live with them and communicate with them by thought processes.'

The chief of police, after giving the little doctor a rundown of the case, asked him, 'How do you think you might be able to help?'

Langsner thought for a moment. 'I should like to attend the inquest. That will put me in contact with all the principals in the case.'

It was arranged that he would sit at the press table and the little doctor's queer appearance, with his black suit and long unkempt hair, caused some sidelong looks from the reporters.

After the jury had given their verdict – that the four people had met their deaths by gunshot wounds, by some person or persons unknown – the police officers and Dr Langsner held a conference in the small police station at Mannville.

Mike Gier turned to the little doctor. 'Do you think now that you may be able to help us?'

'I can tell you the name of the murderer.'

The police chief registered surprise. 'Go on.'

'The murderer's name is Vernon Booher.'

Leslie shot a significant look at his superior.

'When a man commits a crime like this,' explained the little doctor, 'he knows he has offended against society and feels guilty. The circumstances of the crime come to fill his mind and he can think of nothing else. It is not difficult to detect this.'

'Is it possible,' asked the police chief, 'that his mind may be concentrating on something that he does not want us to find?'

'You mean the rifle? Oh yes, I can tell you where that is.'

'You can?' Mike Gier hitched his chair forward and there was a gleam in his eye.

'Yes. I'll take you to it if you like. But not now.' He passed a hand across his forehead. 'I'm feeling very tired. Tomorrow. We'll go out to the farm and I'll show you where it is.'

The next morning quite a party assembled at the now deserted Booher farmhouse on the top of the hill. Mike Gier and Sergeant Leslie and several more policemen were there, anxious to watch the little doctor at work.

Far from being disconcerted by the number of eyes watching him the little man looked as if he were enjoying it. He began at the back of the house, walking up and down like a tracker dog sniffing for scent. Then he lifted his head and looked round. The policemen waited with bated breath.

The little man set off at a fast trot, closely followed by Sergeant Leslie. Langsner stopped suddenly and lifted his head as if he had just heard something, then off he went again this time at an angle to the first direction. This happened a few times and Leslie realised that the little doctor was zig-zagging about a general direction which went towards some thick brush a hundred and fifty yards from the house. He allowed himself a little smile because he and his men had already searched that area thoroughly. But when they finally reached the brush Langsner suddenly disappeared into the dense undergrowth.

'Here it is,' came the little man's high piping voice.

Sergeant Leslie pushed through the shrubs and trees and found the little doctor standing by the side of a large bush. He was looking down into the long grass by his feet.

There, partially concealed by the grass, Leslie could see the butt end of a rifle. 'Well, I'll be damned!' he said.

When the weapon was retrieved it proved to be a .303 Ross Sporting Rifle, exactly the gun that Stephenson had said was missing from his house. Ballistic tests later showed that it was indeed the murder weapon.

To say that the policemen were staggered would be an understatement. Although they had gone along with the experiment, none of them had really expected that the little doctor would be successful. Now they looked at him in awe.

On the way back to Mannville in the car, Dr Langsner turned to Mike Gier. 'I don't want to appear to be telling you how to do your job,' he piped, 'but if I could make a suggestion about the case?'

'Please. Feel free to suggest what you like.'

'I believe that you are holding Vernon Booher as a material witness?'

'We are, but now that we have the gun we shall

almost certainly charge him with murder. You see there's the possibility of fingerprints on the gun.'

'I'm sorry to disappoint you there,' remarked the little doctor, 'but I don't think you'll find any fingerprints. Vernon wiped them off very carefully and still thinks about what he has done. But do not despair. I have a suggestion.'

The result of this was that a little later Dr Langsner sat on a chair outside Vernon Booher's cell. The little doctor leaned forward to stare at the young man through the bars. At first Vernon tried to strike up a conversation with the doctor, but Langsner would not reply and continued to stare implacably at him. Eventually Vernon became angry and turned his back. After about an hour the doctor got up and bidding Vernon good day left the cell.

About half an hour later Booher sent a message that he wanted to see Detective Sergeant Leslie. He then made a full confession to the murders.

Booher said that he was in love with a local nurse. His mother, who had been a very dominating woman, bitterly opposed the relationship and had ordered the girl out of the house and threatened to ruin her name in the very religious local community by spreading rumours about her if Vernon did not give her up.

According to Booher they'd had a row about it on the evening of the murder. Then his mother had turned her back on him. He had lost his temper, picked up the rifle and shot her with it. Fred had heard the shots and came rushing into the kitchen. Vernon was forced to shoot his brother as well.

As he was going out to dispose of the gun he realised that Bill had seen him with it and he would have to kill him too. After that it was not too difficult to shoot Gabriel, the last remaining witness who could testify against him.

Vernon Booher was brought to trial at the Supreme Criminal Court in Edmonton on Monday, 24 September 1928, before Chief Justice Simmons and a jury consisting of six men. The prosecution was in the hands of Mr E. B. Cogswell KC. Before the beginning of the trial the crown prosecutor reported that the prisoner had asked to be defended by Mr Neil D. Maclean, who was one of the leading defending counsels in the country, but he had no funds to pay the fees, his father having refused to give any money for the defence of his son. Mr Maclean was duly appointed by the court.

The first surprise came when Booher pleaded not guilty, since it had been surmised that after his confession to the police, he would plead guilty.

The second surprise occurred on the afternoon of the first day when Maclean attempted to have the confession ruled inadmissible becuase it had been made while the prisoner was under the hypnotic influence of Dr Langsner. In this trial within a trial the little doctor was called to the witness stand by the defence and admitted that he was capable of hypnotising subjects although he denied that he had hypnotised Booher.

The judge gave his ruling the following morning. He felt that the prosecution had failed to show that Booher was not under hypnotic influence when he made his confession, since it was known that the doctor had visited him just before he made it and it would have been easy to influence a simple farm boy. The judge therefore ruled that the confession was inadmissible.

It was the sensation of the trial. But the prosecution were by no means finished. They produced three witnesses to prove that Booher had been in the vicinity of the Stephenson farm on the Sunday morning when the family were all at church. And the judge did allow, in evidence, several partial admissions by Booher, made when he was in custody. At one stage he had muttered, 'Why did I do it?' and at another he told Constable Olsen that he knew who had done the murders, but refused to elaborate further.

The jury were out for two hours before returning a verdict of guilty. Booher was sentenced to be hanged on the 15th of December.

Maclean, however, appealed to the Supreme Court of Alberta. The appeal was allowed. The reason given was that several technical mistakes had occurred in the trial, although it was intimated that the remarkable circumstances of the trial contributed to the decision. The trial verdict was quashed and a new trial ordered.

This took place on 21 January 1929, before Mr Justice W. Walsh. Again it developed into a battle over hypnotism, the crown bringing experts to declare that a man could not be hypnotised to do anything which he would not want to do ordinarily.

But the real sensation came on the second day, when the Warden of the Fort Saskatchewan Jail, where Booher had been confined before being brought back to Mannville for the inquest and committal proceedings, was called to the stand.

John McLean was asked if he remembered a date in early July.

'Certainly. It was on that date that my prisoner Vernon Booher asked to see me.'

'And for what purpose did he wish to see you?' asked the crown prosecutor.

'As it turned out it was for the purpose of confessing to the murders of his mother, his brother and the two hired hands.'

'Now, before I ask you to repeat the confession in detail,' continued Mr Cogswell, 'can I ask you when this occurred in relation to the inquest.'

'It was definitely before the inquest.'

'And had the prisoner been in contact with Dr Langsner?'

'He had not. Dr Langsner never visited the prisoner in Fort Saskatchewan Jail.'

So this confession must have been the first, and it had been made before he had been seen by Dr Langsner in Mannville.

In the confession Vernon Booher expressed regret that he had killed the two hired hands, but not that he had been responsible for his mother's and brother's death, as they had conspired against him to break up his affair with the nurse. In this the confession differed slightly from the one he had made to Sergeant Leslie.

This time the jury deliberated for five hours before they shuffled back into court and gave their verdict. It was guilty.

Vernon Booher was hanged in Fort Saskatchewan Jail on 24 April 1929.

Dr Langsner got his wish of travelling to be with the Eskimos. And some time later he was with them when he died, in a small hut on the outskirts of Fairbanks, Alaska.

5

A Way with Women

'Ah ha! So you've come,' said Madame Cuchet, holding the door open and looking down at the small man standing on the doorstep outside. 'Come in and I'll hear what you've got to say before I call the police!'

She turned, swept down the hall like a ship in full sail, and entered a small sitting room on the right. Taking up a position in front of the fireplace her floor-length skirts almost concealed the empty grate. She motioned the small man to sit. But he shook his head and stood before her tensely.

In his late forties, he was some ten years older than Mme Cuchet. When he removed his bowler hat he revealed an almost completely bald head, and with his small and thin figure he did not look very impressive. Yet his thick dark beard jutted out aggressively and his black eyes stared without blinking and his posture was not in the least submissive.

'You do me an injustice, Jeanne,' he said quietly yet in a rather high-pitched voice.

'Do you an injustice?' flared Mme Cuchet, her eyes flashing. 'You take all my money – after promising to marry me – and then run off and leave me without a sou! And you think that's an injustice to you?'

'Jeanne, I didn't take all your money. I took 5,000

francs and you can have it back at any time. Any time you say. All I did was to reinvest it for you. But I'll return it if you wish. Although withdrawing it all again so soon will entail a certain loss. These investments take a little time to realise their full potential.'

'I don't know anything about that! All I know is that as soon as you got your hands on my money you disappeared. You left me with nothing. After I'd furnished this place – with my money – and paid the rent.

'But what really upset me was when you'd gone and I'd heard nothing from you for days and days and I decided to open that box you left behind in the attic. What did I find? That you'd been corresponding with other women and not only that, but you have a wife and five children living in Clichy!'

The small man took a pace forward, but Mme Cuchet backed away. 'Jeanne,' he said. 'Listen to me. I admit I have corresponded with other women, but if you look at the dates on the letters you'll see that it was before I met you. I really am looking for a woman to share my life.'

'But you already have a wife! And children too!'

'I'm divorcing her.'

'I don't believe you! I don't think you would have come back at all if I hadn't found that accommodation address you use and written to you that I was going to go to the police and have you arrested for cheating me out of my money.'

'It's not true, Jeanne. I was coming back to you. I gave you an expensive engagement ring, didn't I?'

Drawing of Deeming from a
photograph

Vernon Booher

Scene of Booher murders

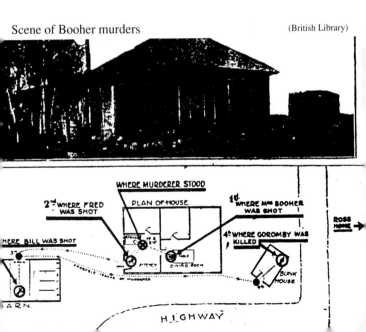

WHERE MURDERER STOOD

2ⁿᵈ WHERE FRED WAS SHOT

PLAN OF HOUSE

1ˢᵗ WHERE Mʳˢ BOOHER WAS SHOT

ROSS HOUSE →

WHERE BILL WAS SHOT

4ᵗʰ WHERE GOROMBY WAS KILLED

BUNK HOUSE

DINING ROOM

KITCHEN

BARN

HIGHWAY

Landru and some of his victims

(The Hulton Picture Company)

Fragments of human bones, press studs and corset hooks found in Landru's stove

(Syndication International)

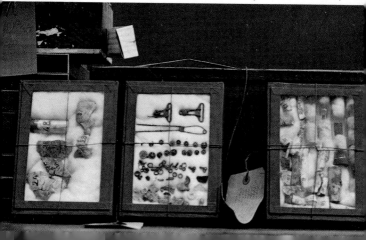

General view of courtroom at Landru's trial

(Syndication International)

Stephen Bradley arrested in Colombo

(Associated Press)

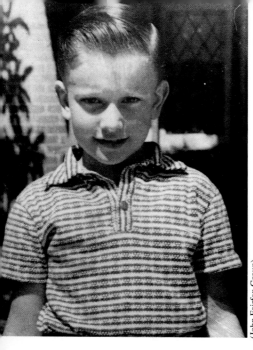

Graeme Thorne

Route Graeme Thorne took

WHERE BOY LIVES

O'BRIEN ST.

BOY D'
REACH

EDWARD ST.

WELLINGTON ST.

George O'Brien

Hootchikoo detachment

Frame of tent-cabin

View of the Yukon River looking upstream from   where the bodies
went into the water

Fred Clayson

William Podmore

Vivian Messiter

The outside gates leading to the garage in which Messiter was foun

'But that was a cheat and a lie!' Mme Cuchet tossed her head. 'You were already married!'

'I know, dearest. I know. But I was afraid I would lose you.'

The argument raged back and forth. But the small man with the jutting beard had correctly guessed the situation. Mme Cuchet, if she was serious about calling in the police, would have already done so. She was a widow with a sixteen-year-old son, who had been earning her own living since her husband had died. But it was July 1914 and war clouds were threatening. Nobody knew what would happen in the future. So when she saw the advertisement in the newspaper:

> Gentleman, aged 47, earning 4,000 francs a year and with some savings, would like to meet a lady of the same age with a view to matrimony.

she replied. She too was looking for someone to marry.

Although he was unimpressive looking, he wooed her with ardour. He didn't rush her, yet sent long passionate letters and small gifts. And whenever they met he was unfailingly kind and courteous. The perfect gentleman. Eventually he awoke feelings within her which had remained dormant since her husband died. They set up house together in Chantilly, a small town thirty miles north of Paris.

'My relatives still don't like you, you know, Raymond. And André wanted me to call in the police immediately.'

'I shall have to make a special effort with him. He's

only a young boy and it's only natural that he should be deeply suspicious of anyone his mother associates with. I tell you what. I'll go out and buy a bottle of wine. You'll be preparing the evening meal as he'll be home from work soon. If you can spare any I'll stay and have some food with you.'

'But you don't drink wine.'

'So I'll get a bottle of mineral water for myself.'

'You wouldn't like to take André and me out for a meal?'

'Nothing would give me greater pleasure, Jeanne. But I really feel that you and your son have a lot to discuss. About what you want to do for the future. And so, if it's not too much trouble, I'll stay for a bite, then leave and you and he can talk.'

But Raymond didn't leave that evening. And nobody ever saw Mme Cuchet or her son again.

'Here you are then, young Belin, a couple of cases to keep you from getting bored.'

Commissioner Dautel of the Paris Garde Mobile dumped two files on to the inspector's desk. It was 6 April 1919 and the young policeman had only been out of the forces a few months.

'Two missing women,' continued his superior. 'Probably gone off with their lovers, but their relatives are getting concerned. See if you can find out what's happened to them.'

'Their names wouldn't be Collomb and Buisson, would they?'

'Oh, I see. You've been talking to Inspector Adam, have you?'

'It's his case, isn't it?'

The commissioner looked a little uncomfortable. 'Well it was, but I've had to put him on to more important work. And then the sister of one of the missing women came in yesterday and started complaining that we weren't doing enough. So, it's now your case.'

Inspector Belin began reading the bulky files on the two missing women. Then he decided to visit the sister, a Mademoiselle Lacoste, who had been in touch with the police.

She was working as a housemaid in the Rue du Plâtre, a few streets away from the Hôtel de Ville (the town hall) of Paris. When Belin knocked on the front door he was told, by an officious butler, to go to the tradesman's entrance. This door was opened by a stout lady in a white apron.

'I've called to see Mlle Lacoste.' He showed his police identification card.

The stout lady ignored it. 'The mistress does not allow gentlemen visitors, except on days off.'

The inspector sighed. 'This is not a social visit. It's official police business.'

The stout lady condescended at last to look at his card. She handed it back.

'Mlle Lacoste's not in,' she said and started to close the door.

'Please. It's very important I speak with her. It's about her missing sister.'

'Celestine?' The stout lady seemed to soften a little. 'Well, I suppose you could come in and wait.'

Belin followed her into a large kitchen. She motioned him to a chair in a corner of the room.

'I'm the cook. You can sit there, but don't get in my way.'

'Do you know Celestine Buisson?'

'I know all about her. Mlle Lacoste's been able to talk about nothing else for weeks. I know she went off with a chap called Fremyet and was last heard of in Gambais.'

At this the outside door burst open and in rushed a young woman, her hair flying from beneath a pert hat 'Marie! You'll never believe the crowds there are in the—.' She broke off as she noticed the inspector who had risen to his feet.

'This is Inspector Belin,' said the cook. 'He wants to talk to you about Celestine.'

'Oh, does he?' She looked across at the detective and her pretty face had a sour look on it. 'I'm fed up with being interviewed by policemen. Each one wants me to tell the whole story again, so that I must have done it hundreds of times already. And what happens? Nothing! I went to Police Headquarters myself yesterday to see what progress they'd made and they'd done precisely nothing. Anyway, you look too young to be a detective to me. And certainly not as nice as the last one I saw.'

During this tirade Belin's face had been getting steadily redder and when the young woman made her final sally he heard the stout lady burst out laughing behind him. He fumbled in his pocket for his card which he again held out and said from between stiff lips, 'I can assure you, mademoiselle, that I am a detective.'

But the young woman refused to look at the card. 'It could be a forgery,' she pointed out haughtily.

The inspector held on to his temper with difficulty. He withdrew a pocket book, wrote down a number, tore out the page, and held it out to the young woman. 'The last policeman who interviewed you was Inspector Adam. That's his telephone number. Why don't you ring up and ask him if I am who I say?'

'I'm not allowed to make private telephone calls.'

'Go on,' said the cook, who seemed for once to have taken Belin's part. 'I'm sure if you ask, and say it is important, the mistress will allow you to.'

Mlle Lacoste said nothing, but with very bad grace she snatched the piece of paper from Belin's hand and walked from the room.

'You'd better sit down,' said the stout lady. 'It may take some time.'

It did indeed take some considerable time and when Mlle Lacoste returned she looked no better pleased. 'You have been confirmed,' she said shortly.

The interview with her was difficult and when the inspector left the house at about midday he had really only established the facts which were already in his files. Mlle Lacoste had visited her sister at the Villa Ermitage, just outside Gambais, a small town on the edge of the Forest of Rambouillet, some thirty-five miles to the southwest of Paris. She had seen Fremyet, her sister's fiancé, there and described him as a short man with a bald head and a jutting black beard. But after this visit she had heard nothing more from her sister. She had written several times to the villa, but had received no reply and in the end this resourceful and persistent young woman had written to the mayor of Gambais asking for his help. That official had gone so far as to walk out to the villa, but found it shuttered and barred. He had written back to say that he could do no more, but had included the address of the owner of the villa and also passed on the information that another family were enquiring about a lady who had gone missing from the Villa Ermitage, a certain Mme Collomb.

Mlle Lacoste had passed this information on to the police and when they tracked down the actual owner of the villa, who bore no resemblance to Fremyet, they found that he had let it to a man giving an address in Rouen. The address turned out to be false.

It was at seven o'clock that night, while Belin was sitting in his office poring over his files, that he received a telephone call.

He could hear Mlle Lacoste's voice screeching in his ear. 'I've seen him! I've seen him!'

'Seen who, mademoiselle?'

'Why, Fremyet of course!' Her voice was getting higher. 'That two-timing—'

'Calm yourself, mademoiselle. Where did you see him?'

The young lady's voice continued to rise. 'Not half

a mile from here! Do you know I've been trying to get hold of you for the past half hour?'

'I'm sorry, mademoiselle. I've been very busy—'

'I rang and rang, but nobody answered.'

'I was on the telephone on another line. Now if you can just tell me where—'

'You're never going to be able to catch him unless you answer the telephone, are you?'

Inspector Belin considered that his caller was far too excited. He decided to give her time to calm down. 'I'll come round and see you.'

'But madame doesn't like us to have male callers—'

'In a few minutes,' said Belin and put the phone down.

A short time later he confronted a slightly calmer Mlle Lacoste in the kitchen of the house where she worked, with the cook and a male servant looking on and listening avidly.

'Well, I'd gone on a shopping errand for my mistress,' said Mlle Lacoste. Her chest was rising and falling jerkily as if she had been running. 'And I was in the Rue de Rivoli when, coming towards me, I saw Fremyet.'

'You're sure it was him, mademoiselle?'

'Of course I'm sure! I'd recognise that jutting beard and that undersized body anywhere. And do you know? He had a lady on his arm as bold as brass! Taller than him of course. Well, you'd practically have to be a midget to be smaller than he is.'

The stout lady tittered.

'And did you not think, mademoiselle, to get a policeman and put the man in charge?'

'Get a policeman! There's never any around when you want them! Anyway, he walked right past me with not a glance in my direction. So I turned round and followed them.'

There were mutters of approval from the two servants.

'I nearly lost them several times in the crowds. Then I saw them go into a china shop. It was the "Lions de Faïence" I think. I crept up as close as I could.' She paused for effect and the cook and the manservant leaned forward in anticipation. 'And I heard them order a dinner service. Then I heard him ask for it to be delivered!'

'Did you manage to hear the address?' Belin couldn't keep a note of excitement from his voice.

'No, but I saw him give the assistant a card.'

The inspector jumped to his feet. 'Mademoiselle, I congratulate you! That was brilliant! All I have to do is to get hold of that card and we will have M Fremyet in custody within the hour!'

But Mlle Lacoste suddenly looked crestfallen. 'He saw me – I think.'

'He saw you?'

'I followed them out of the store, you see, and up to the Place du Châtelet, where they got on a bus going to Montmartre. I tried to get on it too, to follow them, you see. But he was on the platform and turned round and saw me.'

'Do you think he recognised you?'

'Well, I . . . yes, I'm sure he did. He didn't say anything, but he looked right at me. So I couldn't very well get on the bus then,' she finished lamely.

'Good Lord,' muttered Belin. 'I must go to the shop and get that address before the hen flies the coop!'

The inspector literally ran down the Rue du Temple to the Place de Hôtel de Ville and then along the Rue de Rivoli until he came to the 'Lions de Faïence'. But when he reached it the large shop was closed.

He raced round to the rear looking for the caretaker's lodge, couldn't find it, and eventually banged on a likely looking door. After knocking and shouting for some time the door was opened a crack, on a chain, and a rough voice said, 'What do you want?'

Belin pushed his identity card through the gap. 'Police. Open up. I want to look through the records in your dinner-service department.'

The man took the card and went away, presumably to find some light to read it properly.

'Hurry, man. Hurry,' called the inspector.

Eventually the man returned and pushed the card back through the crack, but made no attempt to open the door. 'What is it you want?'

Belin breathed hard in frustration and kept his voice calm with difficulty. 'I want to look through the records in your dinner-service department. A suspect has recently ordered a dinner service and it's vitally important that I find his address quickly before he escapes.'

The caretaker, on the other side of the door, seemed to be digesting this information. Then he spoke slowly. 'Sorry, sir, can't let you do that. No one is allowed to go through our records without the permission of the manager.'

Belin compressed his lips, but he knew it would be useless to argue with the man. 'How can I get hold of the manager?'

'Hang on a minute, I'll find you his address.'

The shop manager lived in the northern suburbs of Paris and it was some considerable time later that the weary inspector, travelling by taxi, reached the house. But then his luck seemed to change. The manager was just sitting down to dinner when Belin arrived, but when the policeman explained what he wanted the executive was kindness itself. He pointed out that the person Belin really required was the assistant who served on the counter. And looking up the man's address he got out his own car and proceeded to drive the inspector there. It was some distance away, and the hour was late when they arrived, but Belin felt that he had no time to lose. With the help of the manager he was able to persuade the reluctant assistant to come back with him to the shop.

It was nearly midnight when the inspector and the shopworker arrived. By this time the assistant had remembered the small man with the jutting beard who had bought the dinner service for his fiancé, but he couldn't recall the customer's name. He began searching through the receipts and invoices which had been thrown together into a large cardboard box behind the counter.

He was a long time searching and Belin sat nearby smoking endless cigarettes to ease his frustration.

At last the tired assistant, who was kneeling on the floor beside the cardboard box, turned in triumph. His hand was raised aloft and in it was a white card.

'Here it is!'

The inspector leaped forward and almost snatched the card from the man's hand.

Then his heart sank. On the white pasteboard were inscribed the words: 'Lucien Guillet, Engineer, 76 Rue de Rochechouart, Paris.'

'This isn't the man's name,' said Belin in a weary voice.

'That's the card from the small man with the jutting black beard, the one who bought the dinner service.'

'An alias, I suppose,' murmured the inspector almost to himself, tucking the card away in a pocket.

It was the early hours of the morning when the detective arrived at 76 Rue de Rochechouart. As he had expected, the building was a block of flats. There was really nothing else he could do that night for French law did not permit policemen to search houses during the hours of darkness. Yet he could not go home to bed. His excitement was still high, even though he was desperately tired, and he walked up and down the narrow street, and, when he was too weary to continue, sat down in the porch.

It was six o'clock when he knocked on the concierge's door. The door was opened by an elderly man with grizzled hair, yawning and rubbing the sleep from his eyes. 'What do you mean waking respectable people up this early in the morning?'

'Police,' said Belin and thrust Guillet's card at him. 'I want to speak to this man.'

The concierge took the card and stared at it. 'You're too late. He's gone.'

'Where?'

'How should I know? He moved out last night. Him and his wife.' He said the last word with a sneer. 'Took a load of luggage with them.'

Belin's heart sank. He had been so near. If only that foolish girl had not given herself away, he might have cracked the case which had been puzzling his department for some time. It was probably not all that important a case, but at least he would have shown himself capable of succeeding where others had failed.

'He didn't leave a forwarding address, I suppose?' asked the detective.

The grizzly-haired man laughed at the look of hope on the inspector's face. 'Of course not.'

Belin turned away.

'Wait a minute,' said the concierge.

The detective turned back.

'He did say he might be back in a few days.'

Belin haunted the cafés and bars in the little streets at the bottom of the hill in Montmartre, below the Basilique du Sacré Coeur, in the succeeding days. In between times he read the files until he could repeat them verbatim. And slowly he came to the conclusion that the cases might be much more serious than they looked on the surface.

One day he was summoned to his superior's office.

'Don't seem to have seen you around the place these last few days, Belin,' said Commissioner Dautel.

The inspector explained what he had been doing.

'Don't you think you're going overboard a bit on these two cases? You've got plenty of others, which you seem to be neglecting.'

'But it could be very important to catch this Fremyet. I'm convinced he's done away with one woman and possibly two.'

'Now, you've no proof of that, Belin. I've read the files too and there are indications that both Mme Collomb and Mme Buisson have gone abroad. One to Algeria and the other to England.'

'I admit, sir, that's where they said they were going. But they were both leaving with a man. I'm convinced that it was the same man, Fremyet, and yet he's recently been seen in Paris with another woman.'

'Again, you've no proof it was the same man in each case and only the word of one witness, and a young woman at that, that he is back in Paris.' It was plain that the commissioner was becoming irritated with Belin's persistence. 'I'm sorry, but I shall have to insist that you drop this case and concentrate on your others.'

'But sir!'

'I'm sorry. There's no more to be said!'

But Belin did not drop the case entirely. Instead he adopted different tactics. While hanging around the Rue de Rochechouart he had made friends with the concierge, by dint of buying him beer at the bar across the street. Now he took to relying on the man to keep watch, dropping in to the bar during the evening to buy him a drink and enquire if Fremyet had come back.

It was late one Friday evening when he arrived at the bar to find the concierge not in his usual place. He looked around then went to the counter to order a drink.

The outside door opened and in came the elderly man. He sidled up to Belin. 'He's come back!' he said hoarsely.

Again the inspector was in a quandary. Since it was dark he had few powers left to him. On the other hand he didn't want to go away in case Fremyet slipped out of the flat again. So he spent the better part of the night sitting on the mat outside Fremyet's front door, occasionally having to retreat upstairs when he heard a late arrival coming up the stone steps.

At eight o'clock in the morning he sent the concierge to Brigade Headquarters for assistance and was joined by one of his colleagues with a gendarme.

'We've got a car outside,' reported his colleague. 'I hope you've got a warrant for this Fremyet or Guillet, or whatever he calls himself?'

Belin nodded.

'You know we've got nothing concrete on him, don't you?' persisted the other detective. 'We can only take him in for questioning. We can't go searching his apartment.'

'Yes, yes,' muttered Belin. 'I know all that.'

'What if he won't open the door? We can't force him to, you know.'

'I've thought about that,' said Belin with a smile.

'I've been looking through the local newspapers while I've been waiting for him to come back and I came across an advertisement from a certain M Guillet offering a car for sale. I'm guessing that it's the same man. I'm going to pose as a prospective buyer.'

'I only hope it works.'

They knocked on Fremyet or Guillet's door. There was no reply. Belin kept on banging until his knuckles were sore. Eventually a sleepy voice came from the other side of the door.

'Who is it?'

'I've come about the advert for the car.'

The high-pitched voice came again. 'Come back later. I'm not even dressed.'

'Can't. I'm on my way to work. But I've got the money here and we can close the deal if you're quick.'

There was a reluctant silence. But the lure of money was too great. There came the sound of bolts being drawn and the door opened a few inches. The two detectives saw a small man with a bald head and a jutting beard, standing in his pyjamas. They leaned forward on the door and pushed their way in.

'What is this? Who are you?'

'Police.' Belin pulled out the warrant and showed it, but not too close, as it was made out for Fremyet not Guillet.

The little man began to bluster. 'You can't break into my house like this!' His high voice was rising in anger.

Suddenly from a room beyond came a woman's scream.

'Damn you!' shouted Fremyet at the police officers and he turned and rushed into another room. The two detectives followed and saw him sitting on a bed cradling a young woman in his arms.

'I'm sorry, sir,' said Belin, 'but you and the lady will have to get dressed and come down to headquarters for questioning.'

'All right,' said the small man, in a quiet voice, stroking the woman's hair. 'We'll do what you want if you'll get the young lady a drink of water.'

Belin went to get the drink while his colleague and the uniformed gendarme kept watch on the pair.

When Fremyet and his pretty young girlfriend had got dressed, Belin said to his colleague, 'Will you take them down to headquarters?'

The other detective looked anxiously at Belin: 'Aren't you coming?'

'I'll follow you down.'

The detective hesitated for a moment, then shrugged his shoulders and went off with his two prisoners.

Belin began to search the apartment. The French police were allowed twenty-four hours in which to interrogate a prisoner. In that time they had to build up a case against the suspect. Then the person was taken to prison, where he remained until his trial, and in all subsequent questionings he was allowed the services of a lawyer. Belin knew therefore that he had very little time to get some evidence on the man known as Fremyet or Guillet.

The search turned up nothing but a fragment of a letter, in a coat pocket, addressed to someone called

Landru, a common enough name and one which conveyed absolutely nothing to Belin.

He followed his colleague to the Sûreté in an apprehensive state of mind, but was met with a beaming smile.

'I think we're on to something at long last,' said the detective.

Belin looked puzzled.

'As Fremyet was getting into the car,' continued the colleague, 'he tried to slip something out of his coat pocket and drop it on the ground. But I retrieved it.' He held up a rather battered-looking notebook. 'And in this are the names of Mme Collomb and Mme Buisson!'

Fremyet refused to say anything about the two women and when asked to produce identity papers replied that he had been born in Verdun. Everybody knew that the town had been almost completely destroyed in the last war and all records of the people born there – which in France are kept at the place of birth – had been lost.

The little man proved to be a tough customer and, leaving him to others to interrogate, Belin went to the Prefecture of Paris, which is the police force of Paris alone. They had at the time more complete records of Parisians than the Sûreté, the detective force covering the area outside the city.

After hours of patient searching for the various names the little man had used, Belin came across some material under the name Landru. There was a bulky dossier on Henri Désiré Landru, who at the time would be fifty years of age. He had received his first conviction in 1900 for fraud and stealing a bicycle. Since then he had been convicted another four times and imprisoned for terms ranging from thirteen months to three years. But the important thing was that Landru had been convicted in his absence on 20 July 1914, again for fraud. He was therefore already wanted by the police and could be held on that charge while enquiries proceeded on the more serious ones.

There was no doubt in Belin's mind that Landru was Fremyet or Guillet. The photograph in the files matched almost exactly the small bearded figure now being interrogated at the Sûreté, even to the bowler hat which the man had been wearing.

When the inspector returned the prisoner admitted that he was Landru.

'As you can see, Inspector Belin,' he said, 'I was wanted by the police and had to have an alias. But, as to murdering these women you accuse me of, well, that's just ridiculous!'

But inside the notebook Belin found a folded receipt for the rent of a disused stable at Clichy, in the northern part of Paris. Here he found stored a quantity of women's clothing, false teeth and corsets, furniture and household fittings, travelling trunks and several sets of documents carefully filed. Two of these sets referred to Mme Buisson and Mme Collomb, but there were also papers referring to four other women the police had never heard of until then. Tracing the last known addresses of these women revealed that each had gone off with a short bearded man and had never been seen again.

Landru refused to say anything about the women. 'If I have been associated with these ladies,' he said suavely, 'I cannot speak of them. A mistress should be considered sacred. It would be a point of honour not to reveal her name.'

The prisoner had to be taken to Mantes, a town about twenty-five miles from Paris, which was the administrative centre for Gambais, where most of the women had last been seen. Travelling with Landru on the train from Paris, Belin decided to stop off at Gambais and, hiring a taxi, took the prisoner and his escort to the Villa Ermitage just outside the town.

It was a small nondescript house behind a line of trees. Making Landru wait downstairs, watched by a gendarme, the inspector made a quick tour of the place. It was sparsely furnished, but Belin could find nothing suspicious.

He then went outside with Landru. In the garden he came across a small pile of bones.

'Ah! What have we here?'

'Don't get excited, inspector,' said Landru. 'If you look carefully you'll see that the bones are too small to be human. There are the skeletons of three small dogs a lady asked me to dispose of.'

Belin was still searching the ground nearby. 'And what are these loops of wire?'

Landru said nothing.

'I think,' continued the inspector, 'that they were devices which could be used to strangle the animals.'

Landru said slowly, 'What of it? It's the easiest way to kill them.'

'And one of the easiest ways to kill a human being as well.'

But the small man compressed his lips.

'If you've anything to tell me,' persisted Belin, 'you'd better do it now. Remember we shall dig up all this garden.'

Landru shrugged his shoulders: 'You won't find anything. But if you do,' he shrugged again, 'over that wall is an old cemetery.'

It took the police two years to bring Landru to trial. Dozens of officers, Belin prominent among them, ran down leads provided by the notebook which Landru had tried unsuccessfully to get rid of. The document was an account book in which the little man had put down his items of expenditure over several years. His meticulous accounting provided clues to the women he had met and the money he had spent on them. Although he frequently referred to them only by nicknames.

It was near the time of Landru's trial when Inspector Belin reported to his superior, Commissioner Dautel.

'So far,' said Belin, 'we've found a total of 263 women with whom Landru has been in contact. That is, names or nicknames in his notebook and other documents we've found.'

The commissioner whistled in surprise.

'We've managed to trace only about a hundred of these,' continued the inspector, 'and all of them seem to have been his mistresses or casual lovers dating back to early in 1914.'

'What about those we're sure he murdered?'

'Well, sir, we've got to number eleven, including the young son of one of the women. This case was the first, we think. Mme Cuchet, a widow of about thirty who worked in a lingerie shop, and her teenaged son André. Landru, who was calling himself Raymond Diard, met her some time early in 1914 and courted her for some time before she and her son disappeared. And it may well be that since this relationship was the start of his career of murder, so to speak, its features might well point to the reasons why—'

'Yes, yes, inspector. Let's have less speculation and more facts.'

'They disappeared just as the war started,' said Belin in an aggrieved voice. 'Chronologically the next was a lady called Mme LaBorde-Liné, who was the widow of an hotelier and originally came from Buenos Aires. Landru – geography was not his strong point – gave her the nickname "Brazil". She was lost sight of in June 1915, as far as we can tell, at a villa he rented in Vernouillet, on the Seine, just a few miles east of Paris.'

'Yes, I do know where it is, inspector. Go on.'

'Then there was Mme Marie Guillin. She was a bit older than the others, about fifty, and had quite a substantial fortune of some 20,000 francs. She and it disappeared – again at Vernouillet – in August 1915. The next seems to have been Mme Berthe Heon, who came from Le Havre and was included in his notebook under that nickname. She had little money and the reason for her removal remains somewhat obscure.'

'If you ask me, the reasons for killing any of them

are very obscure,' muttered Commissioner Dautel, 'but continue.'

'Well, after Mme Heon came Mme Collomb, who, if you remember, was part of our original investigation. She came from a rather higher social class than the others and has become known as the "woman in the blue silk dressing-gown", since she was seen by neighbours wearing that garment in the garden of the Villa Ermitage at Gambais. She already had a lover when she answered Landru's advertisement.'

'I was going to ask you about that. Did he meet them all through advertisements placed in newspapers?'

'No, not all,' said Belin slowly. 'In fact the next one he disposed of after Mme Collomb, was a young girl of nineteen, Andrée Babelay, a servant who worked in the St Lazare quarter. He picked her up on a Metro platform. She had been crying and it appears he was sympathetic towards her. But he soon tired of her and she disappeared in March 1917 at Gambais.'

The commissioner nodded.

'Number eight was Mme Celestine Buisson,' continued the inspector. 'Her family, including Mlle Lacoste, reported her missing in September 1917 and the concierge where she was last known to be living recognised Landru as the man she went off with. Then there was Mme Barthelmy Louise Jaume, by all accounts a stout, religious lady of forty-two who was not seen after November 1917. She was followed by Annette Pascal, who had a small dress-making business. This lady survived a visit to Gambais, for she described to a friend how Landru looked at her in a most frightening way when they were there. But it didn't prevent her going again and she disappeared in April 1918.

'The last one we know of was Marie Thérèse Marchadier, who seems to have been a very low-class woman. An ex-prostitute, she owned a small hotel in the Rue St Jacques and had a bit of money. It was this lady who took her three dogs with her. These were the skeletons we found in the garden at Gambais.'

Dautel pursed his lips. 'But no bodies?'

'No, sir, we've found no human bodies at all. Although we've dug over the whole of the garden of the villa at Gambais, searched the forest around the town and even dragged many of the deep pools they have in the woods.'

The commissioner drummed his fingers on his desk. 'How do you think he disposed of the bodies, inspector?'

'Very difficult to say, sir. The evidence of the dogs suggests that he strangled his victims, probably with thin wire. But since he's only a little chap and many of them were hefty women I think he must have doped them first. I did find a book on poisons in the villa which looked well used. There's also a large slab of stone in the cellar with a good flat surface. He could have used that as a table on which to cut up the bodies.'

Dautel gulped. 'Then what did he do with them?'

'There's always the stove.'

The commissioner shook his head. 'I've seen that. It's far too small to dispose of a human body.'

'It has a very long chimney sticking out through the roof,' argued the inspector, 'which would create an enormous draught. We tried an experiment. We got it going and put a sheep's head in it. It was completely gone in fifteen minutes!'

'Amazing.' Dautel's eyes opened wide with surprise.

'In the ashes from the stove we also found fragments of bone, which the pathologists tell us are human, some press studs and corset hooks, all metal, but charred like the bone fragments.'

'And impossible, no doubt, to say who they came from?'

Belin nodded his head.

The commissioner sighed. Then after a period of silence, he murmured, 'I suppose the man must be mad?'

'I don't know, sir. The psychiatrists think he's perfectly sane.'

'But,' protested Dautel, 'he made so little money out of all these murders.'

'Only a total of 40,000 francs in four years,' agreed Belin. 'I think he just liked chasing women, but soon got fed up with them once they were living together.'

'But why kill them?'

'You have to remember, sir, that he was in constant danger of being picked up by the police. He was wanted for a fraud committed in 1914 and had been convicted and sentenced in his absence. And the sentence was to be transported to Devil's Island. At his age he would hardly have survived that, so I suppose it's not too surprising he took care not to be caught. And having once started on his career of murder he found he couldn't stop.'

Landru was brought to trial in November 1921 at the Versailles Assize Court. For ten days volumes of paperwork were produced in evidence and a parade of witnesses entered and left the box. The verdict of guilty was given on the 30th of November and he was sentenced to death. He faced the guillotine in the early morning of 25 February 1922.

6

Cypress and Pink Mortar

It was at about 7.30 on the evening of 14 June 1960, when there came a knock at the door of the Thornes' ground floor flat in Bondi, near Sydney, Australia. Mrs Thorne answered the door.

In the light from the hall she saw a short man standing on the front step. He looked to be about forty and was rather plump with dark greasy hair.

'Good evening, madame,' said the man politely with a faint foreign accent. He took out a black notebook and flipped over the pages. 'Can you tell me if a Mr Bognor,' he looked at the book again, 'or Bailey lives here?'

Mrs Thorne shook her head.

Behind her, from the flat, came the voice of her husband: 'Who is it, Freda?'

The short man spoke again. 'I'm an enquiry agent. It's – er – a husband and wife matter. You know, a bit confidential.'

Mr Thorne appeared behind his wife in the hall.

The caller consulted his notebook again. 'Can you confirm that your telephone number is 30–7113?'

Mrs Thorne looked shocked. 'However did you know that? Our telephone hasn't even been connected yet.'

'But you have received a letter from the Post-Master General telling you the number?'

Mrs Thorne could only nod dumbly.

The man looked smug. 'We have ways of finding these things out. So you confirm that nobody of the name of Bognor lives here?'

'You might try upstairs,' said Mr Thorne. 'Mrs Lord is in the top flat and she's lived there twenty years or more. She might know if Bognor ever lived here.'

'Thank you very much,' said the man and turned away.

Mrs Thorne closed the door behind him. 'I don't like it, Basil. Do you think we ought to tell the police?'

'Good Heavens, Freda. Whatever for?'

'Ever since you won that money, I've been on edge. First it was the begging letters. Now it's funny callers. How did he know our telephone number when we're not even connected yet?'

'We may not be connected, but we have a number. He probably just rang up directory enquiries.'

'I'm sure people are just looking to burgle us.'

Basil Thorne put his arm round his wife's shoulders. 'Will you stop worrying? He's probably quite respectable. But just to ease your mind I'll have strong locks put on the doors and some secure window fittings made.'

'I'm beginning to wish you'd never won the money.'

Basil Thorne had won £A100,000, about £75,000 – in those days a very large amount of money – in the State of New South Wales Opera House Lottery, which helped towards the building of the famous Sydney Opera House.

About a fortnight later, on Thursday, the 7th of July, Mr Thorne was away on a business trip. Even though he had won all that money he still continued with his old job as a commercial traveller, working for his father-in-law, preferring, as he told reporters, not to squander the money, but to use it for the benefit of his family. Mrs Thorne was washing up the breakfast things after seeing her son Graeme off to school. There came another knock at the door. This time it was Mrs Phyllis Smith.

'Isn't Graeme going to school today?' she asked.

Mrs Thorne looked surprised. 'Of course he is. He left at the usual time, 8.30.' She looked at her watch. 'About half an hour ago.'

'Well, he wasn't outside the shop where he usually waits. One of my boys went into the shop and the man said he hadn't seen him this morning.'

A cold shiver ran through Mrs Thorne, but she put a brave face on it. 'Do you think he's got another lift to school?'

'It's possible.' Mrs Smith chewed her lips in perplexity. 'I tell you what. I'll run my brood up to school and see if he's there.'

Mrs Thorne thanked her, but couldn't resist adding, in her anxiety, 'You will let me know, won't you?'

Mrs Smith drove her own two grey-blazered boys out to Scots College, the prestigious school in Belleview Hill, which Mr Thorne had also attended. She was back in half an hour and breathlessly gasped out her news.

'He's not there!'

Freda Thorne's face went white. 'I'm going to call the police.'

'So soon?'

'I'm very worried. It's not been the same since we won that money. I don't want to take any chances.'

A little later that morning Sergeant Larry O'Shea of the Bondi police had arrived and was sitting in the lounge taking notes when the phone rang.

'Is that you, Mrs Thorne?'

Freda Thorne did not recognise the voice, which had a foreign accent.

'Is your husband there, Mrs Thorne?'

She had a sudden foreboding and her hand began to shake. The sergeant, who had heard the voice on the phone quite clearly, leaped to her side and took the phone.

'I'm her husband,' he said with great presence of mind.

'I have your son, Mr Thorne. I want £25,000 cash by five o'clock this afternoon.'

O'Shea was appalled. He must have been one of the few people who had not heard that the Thornes had won a lottery. 'How am I going to raise that kind of money?'

'You've plenty of money. And you've plenty of time before five o'clock. I'm not kidding. If I don't get the money by five I feed the boy to the sharks.'

'How will I contact you?'

'I contact you.' The man hung up.

The police rapidly went into action. Pictures of eight-and-a-half-year-old Graeme Thorne were shown to neighbours and door-to-door enquiries begun.

The boy had left his own house in Edward Street at 8.30 and walked round the corner into Wellington Street. This is crossed first by Francis Street and then by O'Brien Street. Graeme was seen by a playmate in Wellington Street in his grey school uniform and carrying a school case with his name on the corner in gold letters.

It was his custom to go into the shop on the corner of Wellington Street and O'Brien Street, buy a packet of potato crisps, and then wait outside the shop for Mrs Smith to pick him up in the station wagon. But that particular day he never arrived at the shop. He must therefore have been abducted in Wellington Street.

When Basil Thorne flew into Sydney Airport at one o'clock in the afternoon that day he heard a call for him over the loudspeakers and the police told him his son had been kidnapped.

The public were stunned when the news broke. It was the first kidnapping of a child for money in the history of Australia. Television stations carried extra bulletins, showing pictures of the boy and the area where he had disappeared, and the chief of the Criminal Investigation Branch appeared on TV. The Commissioner of Police, Mr. C. J. Delaney, made an appeal on the radio for the safe return of the child and also for co-operation from the public. Even the State Prime Minister, Mr Heffron, described it as an appalling occurrence and emphasised that it was the duty of everyone to give the police every assistance.

The police did not lack offers of help. During the first night some 400 calls were made to the police, many of them with reports that the boy had been seen in cars with various people from one end of the state to the other.

One report which sounded significant, however, came from a young man, Cecil Denmeade, and his fiancée. They had been driving along Francis Street, where the girl lived, on the morning of the kidnap at about 8.30, when they saw a car parked awkwardly at the intersection of Francis Street and Wellington Street. Anyone walking along Wellington Street would have had to detour round the car. Denmeade saw a man, wearing a gaberdine raincoat and a brown felt hat, get out of the car.

The young man's fiancée also saw the driver and she recognised him as being someone she had seen hanging around Wellington Street earlier in the week.

Denmeade was questioned closely about the car. He hadn't noted the licence number, but described it as an iridescent blue 1955 Ford Customline. And he stuck to his identification even when he was asked to pick out the vehicle from many pictures of similar cars.

With evidence as definite as this the police quickly took up this new line of enquiry. A list of all 1955 Ford Customline owners in the state was compiled. It came to 5,000, and a start was made in interviewing all of them.

The day after the kidnap, a Friday, Graeme Thorne's

school case was found. It was discovered by an elderly man pottering around looking for bottles in the scrub bordering one of the main highways, the Wakehurst Parkway, which leads north out of Sydney. The case was empty, but was easily recognised because of the boy's name embossed on the corner.

Immediately a massive police operation was mounted. All police leave was cancelled and an intensive hunt was begun in the area where the case had been found. A shoulder-to-shoulder search of the bush went on over the weekend amid the torrential rain of the Australian winter.

Then, on the Monday, a little further north, but still in the vicinity of the Wakehurst Parkway, some clothing belonging to the boy was found. His Scots College cap, a plastic raincoat, some school books and scraps of paper with Graeme's writing on them were discovered scattered about in the bush.

The paper was quite dry, and yet it had rained heavily over the weekend, which meant that the articles could only have been dropped very recently. But though motorists were stopped on the highway and questioned, and householders living nearby were interviewed, no sightings were found of a car stopping in the vicinity or of anyone behaving suspiciously.

The investigation seemed to have ground to a standstill. The Thornes received many more telephone calls purporting to come from the kidnapper but they were all proved to be false. The interviewing of Ford owners went on, but this too turned up no leads to the kidnapper.

firmed that the grains were indeed mortar, coloured pink.

'All we have to do now,' muttered Clarke to himself as he left the building, 'is to find a house with pink mortar.'

But in Seaforth alone there were hundreds of houses with pink mortar.

On both sides of the rug and also on the back of Graeme's jacket and trousers, there were animal and human hairs. Samples of these were passed to Dr Cameron Cramp, at the office of the Government Medical Officer, who specialised in hair comparisons.

He found that there were at least three kinds of human hair and a large number of animal hairs. The latter were reddish in colour and Dr Cramp guessed that they came from a Pekinese dog. He confirmed this by comparing them with hairs from no less than ninety dogs of this breed. There was a good chance that the murderer owned a dog of this type.

There was a considerable quantity of plant material associated with the body as well. Fragments of leaves and stems, seeds, fruit and other plant particles were obtained from the rug, the scarf and the boy's clothes. These all needed to be sorted out and classified to see if they would give any clues as to where the body might have lain.

Sergeant Clarke first consulted a botanist and after going out to the vacant lot in Seaforth and examining the vegetation near where the body was found the scientist was able to confirm that a considerable quantity of the vegetable matter had come from that area. But there was some debris which hadn't. It was vital to classify this as well.

But the botanist shook his head. 'I'm afraid the classification is a bit beyond me. I suggest you call in Dr Joyce Vickery of the Royal Botanic Gardens in Sydney. She's been concerned with the classification of plants at the National Herbarium for more than ten years. She might be able to help.'

It turned out to be a mammoth task. Dr Vickery had to ask for assistance from her colleagues to sort out the thousands of pieces of plants in the samples, many of which had to be sectioned and examined under a microscope to determine the internal structure of the fragments before they could be identified. It was thus the middle of September before Clarke received a call from Dr Vickery. He hastened to the Botanic Gardens and together he and the scientist walked among the shrubs and trees.

'I'll cut it short for you,' said Dr Vickery, 'since you'll get my report by post. The important thing is that there are considerable quantities of material from two types of cypress trees on all the clothing and the rug. The first is the Sawara cypress and the second is the Smooth Arizona cypress. Now, the Sawara is quite common in suburban gardens in the Sydney area, but the Smooth Arizona is rare. I would say that you want to look for a garden with these two types of cypress trees close together.'

Sergeant Clarke also managed to trace the manufacture of the rug that had been wrapped round Graeme Thorne's body to the Onkaparinga Woollen Company of Southern Australia. But the company had made over three thousand rugs of this type between May 1955 and January 1956 and it would have been an impossible task to trace every one.

The Criminal Investigation Branch thus had to rely on the pink mortar and the two cypress trees. The detectives reasoned that since most of the pink dust was on the boy's coat he must have lain on his back on a surface evenly coated with the mortar. The most obvious thing was the floor of a garage, near the door of which probably grew the two cypress trees.

Late in September two detectives of the CIB, Detective Sergeant Roy Coleman and Detective George Shiell set out to look for the likely house. They carried with them cuttings of the two types of cypress, supplied by Dr Vickery to help with identification, and they began their search in Seaforth. It was tedious work with many disappointments as they found gardens with one or other of the cypresses, but not both, and not all three of the vital elements. But by the end of September they had covered all of Seaforth and they moved on to the adjacent urban area, Clontarf.

Again the tedious trudging round the streets and gardens began. Then on the 3rd of October, Coleman saw a postman in the street they were searching. He stopped him and asked the question he had asked so many times before. 'You wouldn't know a house in this area with pink mortar and two types of cypress trees in the garden, would you?'

The man tipped his hat up and scratched his head.

'I know a house with two cypress trees in the front garden. I don't know if it's got pink mortar.'

'Where is it?'

'28 Moore Street.' He gave them directions on how to find it.

They went there with no great hopes, since they had run down dozens of similar leads in the last few weeks. But when they reached the front gate and looked up the steeply sloping drive, Sergeant Coleman spoke excitedly. 'It has two cypresses!'

'And it's also got pink mortar!'

They hurried up the drive and compared their sprigs, which were now looking a bit withered, with the two trees standing one on either side of the garage door.

'I think these are the ones,' said the sergeant a little uncertainly.

As he was speaking he saw a woman watching him from a front downstairs window. Then the front door opened and the woman came out on to the drive.

'What do you two want?'

Coleman produced his identity card. 'Police. Would you mind opening up the garage?'

'What for?'

'Don't let's be difficult,' said the sergeant. 'I can always get a search warrant.'

The woman said nothing, but went inside and came out with a set of keys. She unlocked the garage doors and swung them back. Coleman stepped inside the empty garage and stooped to run his fingers over the concrete floor. He raised his fingers so that Shiell could see them. They were covered in pink dust.

126

He turned to the woman who was looking on curiously. 'Do you own a Pekinese dog, madame?'

'Certainly not. I don't like dogs.'

'Or a 1955 Ford Customline?'

The woman laughed: 'You've got to be joking. We can't afford an expensive car like that.'

Coleman stood up looking puzzled. 'What were you doing on the 7th of July?'

It was the woman's turn to look puzzled. Then her face cleared. 'Oh, you mean the day the little boy was kidnapped? We didn't live here then. We moved in soon after.' There was a pause as the woman appeared to be thinking. Then she said, 'But the people that lived here before us, they had a Pekinese. And I believe they had a big Ford car.'

'What colour was it?'

'Blue. Sort of a metallic blue.'

'What were their names?'

The woman shook her head: 'I've forgotten. But I expect the people who live next door, the Telfords, they'll be able to tell you.'

Mrs Telford told the detectives that their previous neighbours had been Stephen Bradley and his wife Magda. Both had emigrated from Europe and spoke English with a foreign accent. They, with their three children and a Pekinese dog, had occupied 28 Moore Street for about six months. Bradley had said that he was a Hungarian who had come to Australia in 1950. He worked as an electroplater, but in spite of the rather low-paid job ran two cars, a small German runabout and the Ford. The family had moved out on the day

Graeme Thorne had been kidnapped. Bradley had asked the Telfords to look after some paintings for him as he was afraid they would be damaged by the removals men and had given a forwarding address in Manly. He returned on the 17th of July to pick up the paintings.

'But if he's the man you want,' said Mrs Telford, 'you'd better hurry, because he told me they were leaving Australia soon!'

Coleman and Shiell raced back to headquarters with their news. A rapid canvass of shipping agencies confirmed that the Bradleys had boarded the *Himalaya*, which sailed from Sydney on the 26th of September and after stopping briefly at Melbourne and Fremantle was now on its way to Colombo.

Chief Inspector Windsor, acting head of the CIB, called his team together at Bondi Police Station.

'I want a hundred and ten per cent effort from now on,' he said. 'I'll apply for a warrant for Bradley's arrest and ask the Australian High Commission in Ceylon to request that the Colombo police hold him when the ship docks. Then two of you, Sergeant Bateman and Sergeant Doyle, will have to fly out and apply for extradition. And that may not be easy to get. The Ceylon people are jealous of their rights. If he seeks sanctuary there we'll need a watertight case before we'll be allowed to bring him back.'

Luckily the Telfords remembered the registration number of Bradley's Customline – AYO 382 – and it was traced to a motor dealer in Granville, some sixteen miles from Sydney. Detectives rushed out there to examine the car.

In the boot they found plenty of traces of pink mortar and plant particles which were subsequently identified as coming from the cypress trees on each side of the garage door at 28 Moore Street. They also found an old brush full of dog hairs, which matched the hairs found on the body.

Examination of the ship's manifest showed that no dog had sailed with the Bradleys when they left Sydney. So the dog had either been destroyed or boarded out somewhere. But where? Again the Telfords came to the rescue. They remembered a vet coming to look for Bradley after the family had moved. Mrs Telford couldn't recall the man's name, but remembered he had a Volkswagen truck. A check of all vets in the area came up with one who had such a vehicle and at his establishment was found the Pekinese dog, called Cherie, waiting to be shipped to England. Its hair proved to be the same as that found on the body.

When the police, led by Clarke, arrived at the flat in Osborne Road, Manly, where the Bradleys had gone after leaving Moore Street, they found it empty. But at the bottom of a rubbish bin Clarke discovered a roll of undeveloped film. When this had been processed it showed pictures of the Bradley family on holiday. One showed Mrs Bradley sitting on a rug identical to the one which had been wrapped round the body. And as if to clinch matters, behind the Moore Street house the searchers found a tassel from a rug, which fitted precisely where one was missing on the murder rug.

Mr and Mrs Thorne were able to identify Stephen Bradley, from photographs, as the man who had posed as a private detective and visited their house a fortnight before the kidnapping. And Denmeade picked out Bradley, again from photographs, as the man he had seen standing by the car on the morning of the kidnapping.

On the 10th of October, Bradley was duly arrested by the Ceylon police when the *Himalaya* docked at Colombo, and detained while his family carried on with their journey to England. Four days later Detective Sergeants Bateman and Doyle arrived from Sydney. But it was over a month later, on the 18th of November, that Bradley was finally handed over by the Ceylon courts. The two detectives and their prisoner boarded the plane to Australia the next day.

Bradley chattered for most of the journey, but as they flew over the continent he lapsed into silence. They had nearly completed their long flight when he turned to Doyle.

'I have done this thing with the Thorne boy,' he muttered. 'What will happen to me?'

When they landed in Sydney he wrote a confession. He admitted reading about Basil Thorne's win in the newspapers and visiting them pretending to be an enquiry agent. He also said that for several days he had watched the boy going to school. Then, on the 7th of July, he had parked in Wellington Street and when the boy came along told him that the lady who usually took him could not come that day because she was ill, but that he would take him instead. Graeme Thorne got into his car without demur. Bradley then claimed that he had simply cruised around, getting out near a bridge to phone the Thorne home with his ransom demand. He then drove to his own home in Clontarf. His family had already left, but the removals men had not yet arrived. Bradley told the boy to get out in the garage, then seized him from behind, wound a scarf round his mouth, tied him up and bundled him into the boot of the car. When he returned later in the afternoon he found that the boy had suffocated. He panicked and dumped the body and subsequently the school case and its contents.

Plainly this confession was not entirely true. As Mr W. J. Knight QC, Senior Crown Prosecutor, pointed out at the trial, it was unlikely that the young boy, who by this time must have realised he was being abducted, would sit quietly while Bradley left the car to make the ransom phone call. And Bradley explained the fractured skull by claiming that it must have happened while the boy was in the boot of the car.

There is little doubt that Bradley, a weak and vain character living beyond his means, had read about the Peugeot kidnapping case in France and become convinced he could pull off a similar crime in Australia. But in trying to keep his victim quiet he hit him too hard and the young boy died.

During the trial, which opened in Sydney on 20 March 1961, Bradley repudiated his confession, saying that he had been forced to make it under threats from the police to prosecute his wife. And though Magda Bradley and her son Peter came back from London to testify that the rug had been lost months before the kidnapping, Peter even giving his step-father an alibi for the morning of the crime, the jury did not believe any of them.

Stephen Leslie Bradley was convicted of murder and sentenced to life imprisonment on 29 March 1961. His appeal was rejected and he died seven years later in Goulburn jail of a heart attack. He was forty-five.

7

The Clue of the Broken Tooth

'Are you guys coming or not?' Olsen, the big Swede, turned before he reached the door of the bunkhouse and looked back at the two men standing round the stove warming their hands. The taller, a thin individual, looked down at the shorter man.

'What do you think, Fred?' he asked in an American accent.

'I don't know,' said the smaller man. 'Since it's Christmas Day I was hoping we could stop over here at Ma Fussell's.'

'Well, if you can put up with her food, do so,' shrugged Olsen. 'I'm going to drop in at the police post at Hootchikoo and have Christmas Dinner with my friend Corporal Ryan. And I know you'd be welcome to join us. He has a turkey too and believe me he's a darn sight better cook than Ma Fussell.'

'Maybe he's got a point there, Fred,' said the thin American. 'And since it's not snowing perhaps we ought to keep on the trail. Although we've made reasonable time so far we could easily get held up if it snows.'

'I suppose so,' said Fred Clayson. 'How far is it to Hootchikoo?'

'It's only sixteen miles,' said Olsen. 'We'll be there

by mid-morning if we start now. And it's a nice easy trail along the ice of the river. Except just for one part where there's a lot of islands in the stream and the ice is a bit rough.'

'All right,' said Clayson. 'Wait till I get my bike.'

'You're not taking that thing along?' asked the Swede. 'You can't even ride it.'

'It's only got a broken pedal,' said Fred Clayson defensively. 'I'm sure I'll be able to find a blacksmith somewhere along the trail. And in any case it's useful to put my pack on the handlebars.'

Lynn Relfe, the American, shook his head sadly and Lawrence Olsen rolled his eyes up in wonderment, but neither of them said anything further as they turned towards the door.

As they stepped out from the warmth of the bunk-house the cold of the Yukon winter hit them like a blow across the chest. It was so fierce it felt like fire in their nostrils and brought tears to their eyes, tears which immediately froze to their lashes. They had to breathe with quick short gasps until their noses, throats and lungs got used to the pain.

Each was wearing a pair of thin silk socks next to the skin, then two pairs of thick woollen stockings which came up to the knees and lastly leather moccasin boots which laced high up on the calf. Yet they could feel the cold seeping through to their feet as they crunched across the snow to the Yukon River.

The trail was wide enough in most places for two men to walk abreast and was mostly out on the river ice, some distance from the bank, where the going was smoother. They had to be careful not to hurry for to sweat was to invite disaster. The sweat would quickly freeze and at the least would cause severe frost bite and might even result in death.

As they followed the twisting trail, Clayson and Relfe explained to Olsen, whom they'd met only the previous evening at Fussell's roadhouse at the small village of Minto, that they had left Dawson separately about a week before.

Fred Clayson was in the outfitting business with his brother in Skagway, a port in the Alaskan pan-handle which was the jumping-off point for prospectors joining the Klondike gold rush, which had begun three years before in 1896. He had taken a scow, a large flat-bottomed boat, filled with clothing, down the Yukon River to the boom town of Dawson the previous summer and quickly sold it all.

He had left Dawson on his way back to Skagway on the 15th of December, riding his new bicycle. But at Selkirk, about 150 miles up river, and 20 miles from Minto, he broke the pedal and was unable to get it repaired.

Lynn Relfe, who came from Seattle, had worked at a dance hall in Dawson as a cashier. He had set off a day later, but caught up Clayson, pushing his bicycle, beyond Selkirk and the two men decided to travel together.

Lawrence Olsen was a telegraph-line repair man and he and Relfe took the lead with Clayson, pushing his bicycle, bringing up the rear. As they came up to a place where a tongue of land pushed out into the river, the linesman stopped. He pointed to a scow which had become frozen into the river ice, its contents covered with a tarpaulin. 'That's the Mackay Brothers' cache,' he said.

Olsen continued, 'This is where you've got the islands in the stream. A guy called Powell cut a new trail a few weeks ago. It's two or three miles, across the neck of that land which sticks out into the river. He used it to sledge meat up to Dawson and its usually known as the Pork Trail.'

He pointed to where a faint trail in the snow diverged from the main river line and climbed the bank. 'But I don't know that the going looks all that good to me, today. I think we'll stay on the main trail and see what it's like among those islands.'

The others agreed and they pushed ahead. They had gone perhaps another mile when Olsen suddenly stopped.

'Isn't that a man up there on the bank?'

The other two followed his gaze.

'You're right,' said Relfe, 'and I think he's got a gun in his hand.'

Olsen never turned up for his Christmas Dinner with Corporal Patrick Ryan of the North West Mounted Police and five days later, when the policeman had seen or heard nothing further of his friend, he went to Minto. There he learned that Olsen had indeed stayed on Christmas Eve and had left the next morning with two companions heading for Hootchikoo.

As he made his way back to his police post he came

to the conclusion that since no one had seen Olsen since early on Christmas morning he must have come to some harm; either fallen and broken a leg or gone through some thin ice on the river. But the fact that he'd had some companions with him seemed to make this idea less likely, unless – and here he stopped to consider the unpleasant possibility – these companions had been responsible in some way for harm coming to him.

He began to search the river bank, poking into every snow drift and searching every clump of trees bordering the stream. About midday he arrived at the point where the Pork Trail cut off the Main Trail. Recent heavy snow had almost obliterated it, but he could just see the slight depression in the surface of the snow, which marked the trail beneath, and where trees and scrub had been cleared to make a passage through. He began wading through the sticky snow. If Olsen had been injured, somewhere along here was the most likely place.

Using a pole cut from one of the trees he carefully probed the snow as he slowly pushed ahead, becoming steadily colder and colder as his slow progress prevented him keeping warm. He had reached what he guessed was about half way along the trail, when the low afternoon sun slanting across the snow ahead of him showed the very faint track of another trail, leading off to his right.

Surrounded by trees he now couldn't see the river, and the new trail wound into the forest away from the stream. He turned to follow it.

Ryan hadn't been on the new trail for more than a few minutes when he saw the cabin ahead of him. His heart jumped and he broke into a shambling run through the thick clinging snow. This surely must be the place where Olsen was holed up. But then he pulled up and his heart sank. No coil of smoke rose from the chimney and the snow was piled high against the door.

There was no one alive in that cabin.

Nevertheless Ryan swept the snow from the door and yanked it open. Inside the dim interior he could make out piles of boxes and sacks but no human form lay on the floor. He made a careful search of the small cabin. It was built of logs, but the sloping roof was only a tarpaulin draped over a ridge pole. Inside was a stove, now cold, a bunk and a cased rifle hanging from the ridge pole. When he examined the sacks and boxes he discovered that they were filled with tinned food, most of it labelled 'Mackay Brothers'.

Ryan returned to the Hootchikoo post, having failed to discover the whereabouts of Olsen, but with another problem on his hands. The food in the tent-cabin had plainly been stolen from the cache near the beginning of the Pork Trail. He sent a wire to the police post at Selkirk, down the Yukon River towards Dawson, where they also had been plagued by a series of cache thefts.

It was 3 January 1900, when Constable Pennycuick from Selkirk arrived at the Hootchikoo post. He was an Englishman, tall and thin and with a dedication to duty which sometimes astonished his colleagues in the Mounties. Ryan explained about the tent-cabin and the two policemen made their way there.

When they arrived the tall Englishman stooped to enter the cabin, brushing snow from his parka when he got inside and taking off his mitts so that they hung from the tape around his neck. He gripped his nose with his bare fingers to thaw the ice which had nearly blocked his air passages. Then he went over to the stove standing in the middle of the cabin and squatted to examine it.

After some time he looked up at Ryan. 'I can tell you who this cabin belongs to – Miller and Ross.'

'How do you know that?'

'This stove.' Pennycuick got to his feet. 'It's Miller's. I saw it in his camp at Hell's Gate. Look, you can see where the damper holes have been punched twice. They make a sort of figure eight. I bet there's not another stove like this in the whole of the Yukon.'

'And you think they'd be the likely thieves?'

'Not a doubt about it. I strongly suspected them of thieving from scows trapped in the river ice around Selkirk, but though I interviewed them at their camp, I couldn't arrest them because I hadn't got a warrant. When it finally arrived they'd gone.'

'I reckon they've gone from here, too,' said Ryan. 'When I first came up here, by the looks of the snow, there'd been nobody around for several days.'

'I'll bet they're thieving their way out,' complained Pennycuick. 'Stealing from caches as they go up river and then selling the grub back to roadhouse owners further along the line. I'll send a wire to Tagish, giving their descriptions, and asking them to keep a look-out. They've got to pass through on their way to Skagway.'

'What do they look like?'

'Not very easily distinguished, I'm afraid. They're both English – well Miller might be Irish. He's average height and thick-set, with dark hair and eyes. His partner Ross is about the same height but of a lighter build. They had two dogs with them. One was a yellow and white St Bernard, a great big thing. The other was small and black.'

Tagish was very much a frontier town. A few miles south were the White and Chilkoot Passes, the summits of which were the border between Canada and Alaska. The passes led through the Coastal Range and down into the ports of Skagway or Dyea.

On the 7th of January, Staff Sergeant George Graham of the North West Mounted Police stationed in Tagish noticed a sledge with a police issue buffalo robe on it and nearby a big yellow dog. He questioned the owner, who gave his name as George O'Brien and said that he'd been in prison in Dawson during the summer and during that time the police had lost his robe and given him a police issue one as a replacement. Although the Dawson police confirmed this story they wired back asking that the man should be detained on suspicion of cache theft.

About four weeks later a stocky American with a thick black moustache arrived at the police post at Tagish. He held out his hand to Sergeant Graham.

'Philip Maguire,' he said with a smile. 'I'm a private detective. Come up from Skagway and been retained by Will Clayson, whose brother Fred has gone missing up near Minto.'

'I am aware of his disappearance,' said the sergeant rather stiffly.

'Sure you are. After all it's been in the papers. And not only Fred, but Lynn Relfe and Lawrence Olsen are also missing, aren't they?'

'What is it you want, Mr Maguire?'

'Philip, please. I've got a letter here from Will Clayson in which he asks you to give me every consideration.'

He handed over the letter, but the sergeant was only halfway through it before the brash American butted in again.

'You see this area is like the frontier in my own country. But the difference is that we have shootings and murders every week, whereas you guys keep this place pretty well buttoned up. In fact I can't remember the last time you had a murder up in the Yukon. So when three guys suddenly go missing it sticks out like a sore thumb—'

'Yes, yes,' interrupted Graham. 'But what is it you want from me?'

'Well,' said Maguire slowly, 'the papers are all saying you got a guy locked up here, Tom O'Brien?'

'George O'Brien.'

'Sure, George O'Brien. I hear he's a hard case who's served time at Dawson and made all sorts of threats about what he would do when he got out.'

'We have a prisoner called George O'Brien,' confirmed Graham. 'But he's being held on a charge of cache robbing. We've no evidence that he's got anything to do with the disappearances.'

'Better find some then, huh?'

'Mr Maguire—'

'Phil. Sorry, shouldn't have said that. But he's the obvious suspect, isn't he? Unless you got somebody else in mind?'

'I'm not at liberty to say who we have in mind.'

'Look,' Maguire's voice was persuasive, 'all I want is a little talk with friend O'Brien.'

'I couldn't possibly allow that!'

The American's attitude suddenly changed. His face was still smiling, but his voice had a hard quality. 'Sergeant, I hear that Major Perry, who you'll remember is Superintendent of the North West Mounted Police, has just had a very hard time with the press and as a consequence has appointed Inspector Scarth to take over the investigation. I guess neither of them would be very pleased to hear that you weren't doing everything you could to help solve this case. But the press, on the other hand, would love to hear it wouldn't they?'

Graham breathed hard, but he knew that there was something in what the American said. Although a good many policemen suspected O'Brien, and he had been seen close to where the men had disappeared at about that time, there was very little to connect him with the crime. If Maguire could come up with something, wasn't it worth a try?

'All right, Mr Maguire – Phil. I'll let you see O'Brien, but I can't force him to talk to you.'

And so it turned out. When Maguire came back into the guardroom after seeing O'Brien in his cell he shook his head. 'He wouldn't talk,' he said. 'But there is one other thing you could do for me,' he hurried on, before the other could respond. 'Let me look through O'Brien's gear.'

'Wouldn't do you any good,' said the sergeant, shaking his head. 'I've already been through it three times.'

'Indulge me,' persisted the American.

'All right,' said Graham in a tired voice, 'follow me.' He led the American to a store room where O'Brien's belongings were contained in a number of kitbags. The contents were emptied out on to a table and Maguire, watched closely by the staff sergeant, began looking through the items.

He eventually picked up a long black woollen stocking, with a leather sole, and before Graham could stop him inserted the blade of a pocket knife into the sole and ripped it open. There, revealed, was a hundred-dollar bill.

The sergeant's mouth gaped. 'Well, I'll be damned,' he said.

'Wait,' said Maguire and throwing down the sock took up its mate. The pocket knife soon revealed another hundred-dollar note hidden in the same way as the first.

Graham could only stare in amazement.

Maguire found nothing more incriminating in O'Brien's possessions and he handed over the money with a smile.

'Wouldn't you say that this makes the case against O'Brien just a little bit stronger? After all I bet he was broke when he came out of jail and yet here he is with all this money. Fred Clayson was carrying quite a lot of cash you know and Relfe probably was too.'

'Doesn't prove that O'Brien robbed them, though. He could have acquired quite a bit of money by stealing from caches and selling the stuff to roadhouse keepers as he went along.'

'OK, but it's a start.' A mischievous smile lifted the corner of the American's mouth. 'What say I allow you to claim that you found the money?'

'And what would I have to do for that?' asked the sergeant suspiciously.

'Simply write me a note to Inspector Scarth, saying you think I'm a competent detective and could be usefully employed by the NWMP in this investigation.'

'You mean we should actually pay you?'

'Why not? The Mounties employ dog-team drivers and Indian scouts, don't they? Why not an American detective?'

A few days later Maguire, driving his own dog team and sledge, arrived at the police post in Selkirk. He found Inspector Scarth and Constable Pennycuick just setting out with their dog sleighs for Hootchikoo.

'I can spare you a few minutes only,' said the inspector. 'Come into the guardroom where it's warm.' He took off his mitts and opened the letter which Maguire handed him. 'This is from Staff Sergeant Graham at Tagish?' He read the letter through. 'Well,' he said thoughtfully, tapping the folded paper on the palm of his hand, 'we do need some more men.' He looked across speculatively at Constable Pennycuick who had followed him into the guardroom. 'This is Maguire,

Constable Pennycuick, a private detective from Skagway, employed by Fred Clayson's brother to find him. He wants us to employ him.'

'But he's an American, sir!' said Pennycuick, horrified.

'Sure am. This wouldn't be the Constable Pennycuick,' enquired Maguire of Scarth, 'who had O'Brien – alias Miller – in his hands and then let him slip through his fingers?'

Pennycuick went bright red. 'That's unfair! I couldn't arrest him without a warrant!'

Inspector Scarth laughed, delighted at the tension he had managed to create between the two men. 'He's quite right, Maguire. We don't arrest people in this country without a warrant.'

Maguire stifled the retort he was going to make about them not being able to catch criminals either and merely nodded his head. 'Sure, sir.'

'I think we'll be able to find you a job, Maguire. You and Constable Pennycuick will get on just fine. Take your mitts and parka off and I'll fill you in a little.'

When all three had seated themselves around the stove Inspector Scarth took out his pipe and began filling it. Maguire did the same, while Pennycuick, who was a non-smoker, thought miserably of the fug which would shortly fill the room.

'Do you suspect Clayson, Relfe and Olsen of being murdered?' asked the American.

The inspector nodded his head. 'It's been so long now since anybody's seen them. Even if they were off on some wild gold hunt to a remote region they must surely have heard the furore that's been going on about them by now. No, I think we've got to assume that their bodies are under the snow somewhere.'

'Or under the river ice,' put in Pennycuick.

'Not a chance,' said Maguire. 'They'll be somewhere around that cabin you folks discovered. But I wanted to ask what you had on O'Brien?'

'Not much,' admitted Scarth. 'Constable Pennycuick identifies him as Miller, and his partner Ross we think is a man called Graves – they're both Englishmen and were together in prison. We know they were at Hell's Gate – not far from here – in early December. Soon after that a carter called Powell and his men were cutting the Pork Trail and saw someone with binoculars watching them from the opposite bank of the river. He got a good look at the man because he went up there to a cabin, called the Arctic Express cabin, O'Brien and his partner were using, to ask for some hay for his horses.'

'How could he be sure it was O'Brien?' asked Maguire.

Inspector Scarth smiled. 'Because he had with him a big yellow dog! This means that O'Brien was in the area where the three men disappeared between the 16th and the 19th of December, only a few days before they actually went missing.'

The American shrugged his shoulders. 'Not a lot to go on is it?'

'Listen to this, then. Before Relfe left Dawson a man gave him an odd-shaped nugget of gold. It was a lump about the size of a half-dollar piece, but on one side was another smaller nugget which was trapped inside the first, so that it rattled when you shook it. Relfe was showing this at Fussell's the night before he disappeared. And a watchman on one of those river steamers frozen in near Tagish says that early in January a man tried to sell him a nugget like that. And the man had a big yellow dog with him!'

Early the next day Constable Pennycuick and Maguire set out with their dog teams. They were to stay in the Arctic Express cabin and scout the area. Now that he had signed on the American, the inspector had decided not to go with Pennycuick.

Because Maguire had the superior lead dog he made much better time than Pennycuick and his team, and by the time the constable arrived at the cabin the American had already lit the stove and had a kettle boiling.

'Can't the Mounties afford decent dogs?' he asked slyly as he handed Pennycuick a cup of tea.

'Thanks,' said the Englishman accepting the tea. 'Let's get one thing straight, Maguire. I don't like you and I don't suppose you like me either. But we've got to work together, so I suggest we keep the funny remarks to ourselves.'

'OK, OK. No need to get so stuffed shirt about it,' said Maguire. But plainly he was offended.

They said little more to each other, but went about the chores that needed to be done, like chopping wood for the stove, packing away the stores they'd brought with them, sorting out blankets and bunks and sealing the cracks between the logs forming the walls to cut down the icy blast which whistled through the small cabin.

The next day Pennycuick took Maguire to the other side of the frozen river, showed him the Pork Trail and the tent-cabin, then left him to scout the trails around there while he went back across the river. Some trails had been discovered behind the Arctic Express cabin and Pennycuick's job was to follow these in case they had been made by O'Brien and his partner. They were both looking for signs of bodies having been hidden or any clues as to what O'Brien and his partner had been up to in the area.

They spent several fruitless days floundering on foot on their own, or behind their dog sleighs, through waist-high snow following the faint trails. It was difficult, exhausting work and each man returned to the cabin at night, bitterly cold and tired out and not much inclined for conversation.

But after about a week Maguire returned one night with a triumphant light in his eye. 'Found anything yet, limey?' he said as he took off his sopping wet mitts, squeezed out the water and hung them near the stove.

Pennycuick was too tired to answer. He merely slumped on his bunk and turned his face to the wall.

'Well, it takes a Yank to show you guys how to find things,' continued the American.

This time Pennycuick turned to face him. 'What have you found?'

'You'll have to wait till tomorrow to find out. But

then I'm going to take you over to the Pork Trail and show you the reason why we're here!'

And he would say no more on the subject.

The next day he was equally mysterious. After breakfast they trudged over the thick ice of the river to where the Pork Trail branched off the main River Trail. When they reached the turn-off to their right to the tent-cabin, Maguire gestured with his arm.

'We go on a-ways.'

Again he vouchsafed no explanation and Pennycuick followed him in silence. They'd gone about another quarter of a mile when the American stopped and pointed ahead.

'Just up there there's a fork. The track to the right is the original Pork Trail, which meets the River Trail about another mile or so further on. But this one to the left is newer.'

He led the way along this new trail for a couple of hundred yards then stopped. 'Look there.' He pointed.

Pennycuick saw a tree with a piece cut from the bark. Just beyond this they could see yet another fork in the trail.

'I didn't cut that blaze,' said Maguire.

'Who do you think did – O'Brien?'

'Very likely. Now both of these trails,' continued Maguire, 'lead to the river. We take the left-hand one.'

The track began sloping down towards the river. They were moving through a heavy growth of spruce which prevented them seeing the stream and as they passed they noticed several more blazed trees, obviously recently cut to mark the way. Then the American halted. He went forward cautiously, bent over and began to scrape away the snow carefully in front of him. Then he straightened and stepped back.

'Take a look at that.'

Pennycuick looked over the American's shoulder and saw a patch, about a foot across, of some thick reddish-brown material.

'What is it?'

'My guess is it's blood. And there's another one further up here.'

Maguire led the way a few yards further on and uncovered another of the brown patches.

'I covered them up with snow after I found them to prevent anyone destroying the evidence.'

Pennycuick bent to examine the second more carefully. Then he too straightened.

'I think you're right. It is blood. However did you find them?'

Maguire laughed in a boyish way. 'Tell you the truth it was my dogs found them. I was driving them over the trail when they suddenly went mad. Could smell the blood I guess. I dug down and there they were.'

'They're certainly large pools – if it is blood – and must have come from a man, or a large animal.'

'I've found the murder scene,' said Maguire confidently. 'There's little doubt the men were killed here.'

'But what happened to the bodies?'

'There's no doubt about that either. They were taken back to the tent-cabin, stripped and the bodies dumped in the bush nearby. I've sifted through the ashes of the stove in the cabin and found three moccasin eyelets and a belt buckle. Somebody has been burning clothes in that stove. And why would anybody do that, except to get rid of evidence?'

'Could be,' said Pennycuick slowly. 'There's no bodies around here?'

'No. My dogs would have smelt 'em. Let's go back to the tent-cabin and have another search there.'

They retraced their steps to the first of the blazed trees.

'Where does that other trail go?'

'Down to the river. But it ends abruptly at the top of a cut bank. It's not important.'

Pennycuick frowned. 'It might be. It might just be the place where the bodies went over into the river.'

'That's ridiculous. The bank there's forty feet above the ice.'

The constable smiled: 'I know this river bank better than you do. And where you describe is where the bank is washed away because it sticks out into a strong current. And it's also where there would be a hole in the ice due to the current.'

'I still say—'

'Listen.' Pennycuick put up his hand. And in the quiet they could hear the faint sound of a man shouting. 'I'll bet that's Inspector Scarth and his dog team. He's coming up the Pork Trail.'

'What on earth for?'

'He likes to drop in on people unexpectedly.'

The constable was right. They soon saw the dog team and the man urging the dogs on with his voice and a long whip.

The inspector drew his team in beside the two men and greeted them.

Then he asked, 'Have you found anything yet?'

'Yes, sir,' said Maguire. 'I think you'll be interested in this.' He led the way down to where the blood patches were.

Scarth took a good look at both patches. 'I suppose you think this is blood?'

'Definitely, sir. We could be standing just where the three men were killed.'

'On the other hand, we could not. This could be dog blood, or even from a horse. Anything else?'

'There's a few things up at the tent-cabin,' said a crestfallen Maguire.

'Let's go see, then.'

When they reached the cabin, Maguire somewhat diffidently showed the inspector his gleaning from the stove ashes – the metal eyes from moccasin boots and the belt buckle.

'Hm,' said Scarth. 'I agree it's unusual to burn clothes in a stove, but there's no indication that these came from our missing men. And until we can definitely say that, they're not much use.'

Maguire opened his mouth to protest, but changed his mind. He produced a bottle. 'I found this in the snow outside the cabin.'

The inspector read the label. 'Hudson's Bay Company West India Lime Juice.' He took out the cork and sniffed at the end of the bottle. 'Whisky,' he muttered. 'It might be useful if we can establish where it was bought.' He handed the bottle back to the American. 'But it needs to be properly labelled. Who found it, when and where.'

He motioned the two men to follow him out of the cabin. Then once out among the trees he turned to face them.

'Have you found anything, constable, on the other side of the river?'

Pennycuick shook his head. 'No, sir.'

'It won't do, you know, both of you. You've been here a week and found very little, and even that we can't tie up to either O'Brien or the missing men. We've got a man in custody, who we can possibly charge with cache robbing, but that's all. If we try to pin a murder charge on him it will be laughed out of court and we'll also be a laughing-stock. And on top of that the papers are on our backs – well mine and Major Perry's – all the time.

'What we need, gentlemen, is evidence. Solid evidence which will link O'Brien with the crime. I'll give both of you another week. If by that time you haven't found anything, I'm afraid I'll have to take you off the case and bring in some more investigators. Good day.'

And with that he trudged off to his sleigh.

Maguire and Pennycuick both stood watching the inspector until he had disappeared among the trees. Then the American expressed his displeasure by a sudden snort. He took off his mitts and threw them down in the snow.

'Why that jumped-up, opinionated son of a bitch! I'll be damned if I let him talk to me that way! I quit! Do you hear me? I quit!'

'Now take it easy, Phil.'

Maguire was so surprised to hear Pennycuick call him by his Christian name that he stopped and looked at the constable.

'There's no need to go off at half-cock. Scarth's under a lot of pressure himself. And what he said was largely true. We haven't yet got anything solid to pin on O'Brien. On the other hand you've done very well and we've got to try and build on that.'

'But what the Hell are we going to do?'

'That area where you found the blood pools. I think you're right. It is the murder area. Well, there's bound to be some evidence there.'

'But it'll be covered in several feet of snow.'

'We'll just have to clear it then, won't we?'

'Clear the snow? You're mad! Do you know that, Pennycuick? You're stark staring mad! It would take us from now till the thaw to do it.'

'We'd better get started then, hadn't we?'

And he turned and set off along the trail. Maguire followed reluctantly, muttering to himself about the madness of the English. When they finally reached the blazed tree Pennycuick stopped.

'If we start by removing the snow in a line, say four feet wide, from here down to where you found the blood and then beyond that to the river, what do you say?'

Maguire nodded miserably.

'I'll get a surveyor's chain,' continued the constable, 'and we'll measure all the trails and draw a map. Then anything we find we'll be able to plot its exact position. Shall we get started?'

It was fiendish work. They couldn't risk shovels because of the danger of destroying or removing valuable clues and so all the snow had to be moved by hand, carefully scraping away at the surface and peering intently all the time to make sure they missed nothing. Having to work kneeling in the holes they excavated quickly made them frozen stiff and they had to take frequent exercise breaks to prevent frostbite or simply to avoid succumbing to the intense cold.

They soon found more and more blood spots. And the patches seemed to group themselves into three distinct areas. There was some blood down near the river, some more further up nearer the centre of the trail, then a widespread collection further away still, near the first blazed tree.

'My guess is,' said Pennycuick, 'that the three men were coming along the river trail when someone held them up at gunpoint and forced them to go on to the river bank. Then they were cut down with rifle fire, possibly from two directions. One of the men fell near the river. Someone else was shot down further up, but it looks like the third person made a fight of it.'

'Or a run for it,' put in Maguire.

'Yes, that makes sense. The blood up near the blazed tree looks as if one person was shot several times as he was moving.'

'Pity we haven't found any spent cartridges,' remarked Maguire wryly.

But they eventually did find some cartridges. One Pennycuick discovered in the middle of a patch of blood.

'This makes a nasty picture,' he said.

Maguire came up, took the bloodstained metal tube from him and looked down at the patch of blood.

'Yeah,' he said, 'looks like somebody was shot at point-blank range. Most likely as they were lying helpless on the ground.'

'What calibre is that?'

Maguire turned the cartridge over in his hand. 'I would say it's a .40–82 Winchester.'

'That will fit the rifle found in the tent-cabin,' said Pennycuick excitedly. 'If there was a lot of shooting,' he continued, 'we ought to find marks on the trees.'

And indeed there were places where the wood had been chipped by passing bullets.

Several days later the constable found a screwed-up wad of paper in a willow bush. He carefully opened it out. It was a receipt for meals and accommodation from the Fussell Roadhouse in Minto. Dated the 22nd of December it had been made out to L. Olsen.

Pennycuick gave a whoop of joy which brought Maguire running across.

'This is the first solid evidence,' he said, 'that Olsen was actually here.'

The find considerably heartened the cold and tired men and soon after this the American found a medicine bottle which, from the label, had been Olsen's.

Then Pennycuick made the major discovery of the search, though he didn't realise it at the time.

Raking through another patch of blood with a twig, looking for more cartridges, he unearthed a small solid. Fishing it out he called Maguire over.

Five weeks after the kidnapping, on the 16th of August, some young boys made a gruesome discovery. They were playing on waste ground in Seaforth, an urban area only a couple of miles south of where the school case had been found, when they decided to investigate a largish bundle wrapped in a brightly coloured rug. It had been pushed into a hollow under a boulder and the children had seen the bundle around for some weeks, without bothering with it, but when one started to unwrap it he saw a human arm. He ran to tell his father. The body of Graeme Thorne had been found.

Police from Manly, the nearest town, after a brief examination, got in touch with the headquarters of the kidnapping investigation in Bondi and senior officers were soon on the scene. The Government Medical Officer, Dr C. E. Percy, examined the body before it was moved, but it was so badly decomposed that he was unable to come to any immediate conclusions as to the cause of death. It was removed to the morgue in Sydney where a postmortem was conducted.

The sorrowing parents confirmed that it was their son, although the young lad was easily recognisable since he was still wearing the school uniform he had on when he set out for school.

The boy's arms and legs had been tied with twine and a scarf tightly wrapped over his mouth, presumably to prevent him calling out. There was also an injury to the back of his head which had resulted in a fractured skull. The postmortem revealed that he could have died as a result of the fractured skull, or from smothering with the scarf, or a combination of both. And the indications were that he had been dead for several weeks. Probably he had been killed very soon after the abduction.

The kidnapping had turned into a murder case. But whereas the kidnapping had provided few clues, now there were plenty.

The Scientific Investigation Bureau in Sydney was run by Detective Sergeant Alan Clarke. The department did not employ scientists of its own, but was mainly an organisation for collecting material from the scenes of crimes, which was then passed on to scientific institutes for examination.

The morning after the discovery of the body Sergeant Clarke and his forensic team went to Seaforth. They searched the site inch by inch looking for anything which might have been dropped by the murderer and collecting samples of soil and vegetation near where the body had lain. Then the clothes which Graeme had been wearing and the rug he had been wrapped in were taken to the laboratory for further examination.

On the boy's shoes, the seat of his trousers and the back of his jacket and even on the knotted scarf, they found a pinkish dust. Under the microscope it looked like sand grains. But the police could find no pink sand in the Seaforth area.

Clarke mentioned the problem to a colleague.

'It could be mortar,' said the man. 'The other day I saw someone mixing a pink dye into some mortar.'

The sergeant took samples to the Geological and Mining Museum in Sydney where the curator con-

'What do you think that is?'

The American carefully wiped the bloody mess from the small whitish object and rotated it with his fingers. 'If I'm not very much mistaken it's a tooth. And I would guess it's a human tooth or part of one.'

Another fragment of tooth was found in the sticky pool on the packed snow. This one was smaller, but when cleaned it clearly showed a grey smear of lead, indicating that it had been struck by a bullet.

Although the pair searched assiduously near the tent-cabin they didn't find the bodies, or any sign of them, which made Pennycuick feel that he was right. The bodies had gone into the river under the ice.

This was finally confirmed a month later, when on 30 May 1900, the first of the bodies was recovered. By this time the river ice had all but disappeared and the body was found on a sandbank a mile and a half upstream from Selkirk. There were felt boots on the feet and the marks of bicycle pedals could still be seen on the soles.

On the 8th of June another body was discovered in the river at Hell's Gate, eleven miles up river from Selkirk. This one had visiting cards in the pockets in the name of Lynn Wallace Relfe.

The autopsy, conducted in Dawson by Dr Howard Hurdman and Dr William Thompson, on the second body, established that Relfe had been shot several times. And the broken tooth pieces, which Pennycuick had discovered, fitted perfectly into the skull. This was the plainest evidence that Lynn Relfe had been murdered near the Pork Trail.

Olsen's body was not found until the 26th of June, when an extensively decomposed corpse was found in the river and conveyed to Dawson. It was identified mainly from the teeth and skull, which several men who had known him were able to recognise.

George O'Brien was brought to trial at Dawson on 10 June 1901, nearly a year after the first body had been discovered. He was charged only with the murder of Lynn Relfe, since this was the most complete case which could be brought against him, although the court did allow the introduction of evidence on the murders of the other two men.

The case against O'Brien was entirely circumstantial, but there was a wealth of evidence against him.

Apart from being seen near the Pork Trail by Powell before Christmas, he was seen again actually on the Pork Trail only two days after the murders by a man and his wife who were travelling to Skagway. Then two witnesses were produced who said that O'Brien had tried to interest them, months before the murders, in plans to hold up and rob travellers on the trail. Then cartridges which were found on O'Brien and which fitted the rifle and revolver he was carrying were of the same calibre and type as those found at the scene of the crime.

The jury had no difficulty bringing in a guilty verdict and O'Brien was hanged on Friday 23 August 1901, at Dawson, to the last denying all knowledge of the crime.

His accomplice, and it is most likely that he did not commit the crimes on his own, was never found. Some say that he too was murdered by O'Brien and his body

The boy took hold of the lead rope as if it was his right, and they all followed on to see him bed down the new arrival.

dumped in the river, others that he got clean away. It seems unlikely that we shall ever know the truth.

8

A Burnt Offering

On the night of 30 July 1925, the little town of Walnut
Creek, a few miles inland from San Francisco bay, was
rocked by an explosion. Soon afterwards the sky above
was lit by the light of flames. People tumbled out of
their houses as the smell of burning wafted through the
streets.

One of the first of these was a young man, who ran
out of his front door to look at the fire. 'It's the cellulose
plant,' he called to his mother who was following.
'Better call the fire brigade.'

The house was almost opposite the factory and the
young man could see flames shooting through the roof
of the new two-storey building. Then, as he was standing in the road, he heard the sound of an engine, and
a car, without any lights, appeared out of the gloom
and nearly ran him down. He had to jump for the
pavement and stood gazing after it in surprise.

When firemen from the nearby town of Berkeley
arrived, the flames were already beginning to die down,
to be replaced by thick acrid chemical smoke. Nevertheless, a man pushed his way to the front of the crowd
outside the gates. 'Please, I must go in. Mr Schwartz
may still be inside!'

He was restrained by a policeman while the chief of the Berkeley Fire Brigade, Guy Spencer, was called.

'Who're you?' asked the fire officer.

'I'm Walter Gonzales, the caretaker at the plant. I left Mr Schwartz alone in the laboratory only a short time ago.'

Spencer nodded: 'Where's the lab?'

'On the first floor. But hurry!'

The fire-fighters had just about got the flames under control as some of them battled their way up the outside staircase and smashed in the door of the laboratory with their axes. Sometime later, when the flames had finally been conquered and the building stood gaunt and black against the dawn sky, the fire chief called for Gonzales. The caretaker was led up the now rickety iron staircase and into the almost gutted laboratory.

He found a knot of firemen clustered round a huddled shape on the floor. Spencer detached himself from the group and approached Gonzales. 'Is that him?' He shone a torch on the figure lying among the debris.

The caretaker bent over the blackened form. Then abruptly swung away and began retching in a corner. When eventually he turned back it was to nod his head dumbly.

Later, he was able to explain that the dead man, Charles Henry Schwartz, had been the owner of the factory. A chemist, he had been working on a new, and secret, process for the manufacture of artificial silk. Gonzales had seen him working alone in the laboratory only a short time before the explosion occurred and

Schwartz had told him he could go as he would be leaving shortly himself.

'An accidental spillage of chemicals, perhaps,' remarked Spencer to the sheriff, R. R. Veale, when the two met by the factory gates. 'It caused the fire and the explosion and, since the body was halfway between a lab bench and the door, we must assume that the poor guy couldn't get to the outside door in time.'

'I'll get in touch with the coroner,' said the sheriff.

The next day he conferred again with the fire chief, this time in the sheriff's office. 'There's little doubt that the body is that of Schwartz,' said Veale. 'Although it's unrecognisable, his wife was able to do the identification from a watch and some jewellery we found on it. We also took a detailed statement from Gonzales, in which he said that earlier in the day Schwartz emptied his purse and had coins to the value of $1.73 in it. And we found coins to exactly that amount on the body.'

'Seems conclusive,' said Spencer.

'There's another thing. Mrs Schwartz said her husband phoned her at home at ten minutes to nine and said he would be coming home soon.'

'Yes, that would fit,' said Spencer. 'Most witnesses put the explosion at about nine o'clock. But,' – here he stopped, pursed his lips and drummed his fingers on the arm of his chair – 'there's something you ought to know. I've had another look at the site this morning and I'm not happy about the way the fire started.' He took a deep breath. 'I believe the fire was not accidental!'

'How did you get that idea?'

'Near the bench, or what was left of it, where Schwartz was apparently working, I found six, what I think were torches. They looked as if they had been made from short lengths of stick around which were wrapped some kind of coarse cloth. I think the cloths were soaked in some inflammable liquid and set alight deliberately.'

'I see,' said the sheriff rubbing his chin reflectively. 'That does alter things a bit.'

Later he went to see the widow and was shown into a sitting room at the Schwartz home in Walnut Creek. 'Can you tell me, Mrs Schwartz,' he asked, after he had seated himself on a hard-backed chair, 'if your husband was in any financial difficulties?'

The grieving widow, seated opposite, dabbed at her eyes with a tear-stained handkerchief. 'I don't think so, sheriff,' she sniffed. 'He had some financial backing for the venture, as you probably know. Although he was still doing research on the process to improve it still further. And he was hoping to attract some more funds from local businessmen. Why do you ask?'

Veale's big hands were placed on his thighs and he squeezed his legs in an embarrassed manner. 'There's been some doubt expressed about the cause of the fire, Mrs Schwartz. I'm afraid I'm going to have to ask the coroner to cancel the funeral.'

'Cancel the funeral? Whatever for?'

'So we can proceed with our investigations.'

'Whatever are you talking about, sheriff?' Mrs Schwartz's voice was high.

'Well,' said Veale slowly, 'it has been suggested that the fire was not accidental, which means that your husband's death may not have been an accident either.'

Mrs Schwartz was silent for some time. When she spoke her voice was low. 'You mean somebody tried to kill him? Did kill him?'

'That is one possibility,' said the sheriff carefully.

The widow lifted her chin and sat upright in her chair. The expression on her tear-stained face was grim. 'I see,' she said slowly. 'Well, I can only say that my husband did tell me that there were several people after his secret formula. I suppose it's possible that one of them might have killed him to obtain it.'

She could, however, give no information on who might have wanted Schwartz's secret. The sheriff decided to investigate the chemist's background. He found that Schwartz was thirty-six when he died. Gossip around the town had it that the man had a distinguished record in the First World War. He'd been a French flying ace and there was even the possibility that he had been a spy in the Allied service, as he was known to be a fluent German speaker.

He had worked for various chemical companies after the war until he finally set up in business for himself in Walnut Creek. But apparently he had little money of his own. Most had come from his wife.

Then the sheriff came across another curious fact. Rumour led him to a pretty young woman who worked in a beauty parlour and she admitted to an association with Schwartz. She had even begun a breach-of-promise suit against him.

Sheriff Veale discussed the matter with District Attorney A. B. Tinning and told him what he discovered. 'You see,' said the sheriff, 'although Mrs Schwartz firmly believes her husband was murdered there are other possibilities. He hasn't much money of his own and it could well be that some of the financial backing for his new process was not coming through. He might even have been having trouble delivering on the research. And then there's this breach-of-promise action. He might have decided to end it all and to cover up and make it look like an accident.'

The district attorney nodded his head. 'What's the evidence for it being murder?'

'Well, there's not much, except the suspicions of Mrs Schwartz and the statement of Schwartz's secretary, Mrs Esther Hatfield. She said she saw him put $900 in his pocket on the day of the fire. We've looked very carefully on the body and in the laboratory and although we've found charred letters and other papers, there's no sign of the remains of dollar bills.'

'Seems an awful lot of trouble to go to merely for a robbery.'

'I agree,' said the sheriff. 'But I feel there's a wealth of forensic evidence lying about that we're not actually picking up on.'

'Have you thought about calling in Dr Heinrich?' asked Tinning.

Dr Edward Oscar Heinrich was one of the foremost experts in criminology at the time in America. A professor at the University of California, he had a laboratory at Berkeley and had been instrumental in helping to solve some very difficult cases.

After he had agreed to see what he could do, the criminologist went to the sheriff's office to be briefed by Veale and Tinning.

When the sheriff had outlined the case, Dr Heinrich asked, 'What evidence have you got for identification of the body?'

Veale summarised Gonzales' evidence and that of Mrs Schwartz. 'The watch and jewellery found on the body have also been attested to by many friends of the family. Then the family physician, Dr Alfred Ruedy, has also viewed the body and says that in his opinion it belongs to Schwartz, and finally Schwartz's dentist was able to confirm the finding by virtue of a molar which is missing on the upper right of the jaw and which the dentist remembers removing.'

'Sounds all right,' said the doctor, 'but I'd still like to have a quick look at the body as well as the laboratory. Oh, and could you find out for me what Schwartz had to eat during his last meal?'

The famous criminologist left the sheriff and the district attorney looking very surprised.

During the next few days Dr Heinrich was very busy. He and an assistant went over every inch of the laboratory in the burnt-out factory, examining minute stains under powerful magnifying glasses, scraping up debris of all kinds and sealing it into small packets for later examination at the laboratory in Berkeley. The pair took measurements and made plans and drawings. They finally took away with them an old paraffin lamp, an old sugar bag containing something that looked like coffee, an object resembling a sewing kit, and some charred fragments of paper.

The scientist also consulted the firemen who had been on duty on the night of the fire and spoke to the men who had entered the burning laboratory first and who had reported encountering some choking yellow fumes which had driven them back.

He then went to the morgue and examined the charred body. Soon after this he phoned Sheriff Veale. 'Could you obtain one of Mr Schwartz's hairbrushes for me?'

The mystified sheriff had the hairbrush delivered to Dr Heinrich's laboratory.

Some time later, Veale rang the criminologist.

'Have you managed to determine yet whether Schwartz's death was suicide or murder?'

'Oh, I think we can say quite definitely that it's a murder case. I'm just putting the finishing touches to my investigations and the report should be with you in a short while.'

'You wouldn't care to summarise it for me over the phone would you?' asked Veale, more in hope than expectation.

'No, I wouldn't. But I'll bring it over for you in a few days.'

'Well, that'll be something,' said the sheriff.

'Have there been any further developments in the case?' asked Heinrich.

Veale thought for a moment. 'I don't know,' he said slowly. 'I've just had a report that there's been a break-in at Mrs Schwartz's home. But I don't know if it has anything to do with the case or not. I'm just going to see her.'

A few days later Dr Heinrich was as good as his word and arrived at the sheriff's office carrying the bulky document under his arm.

'My first job,' he said as he sat down opposite Veale and Tinning, 'was to confirm the opinion – or not as the case may be – of the fire chief, that the fire was started deliberately. And I think we can say, gentlemen, that it definitely was. At first I wasn't quite sure how it was done and suspected the paraffin lamp. But after taking this to pieces and examining each part minutely I can safely say that it had nothing to do with the fire.

'I was intrigued by the reports from the firemen of a yellowish choking gas in the factory lab when they first broke in. Chemical analysis of residues I found indicated that the gas was carbon disulphide, which is an extremely inflammable chemical.'

'And you think that this was used to start the fire?' asked the sheriff.

'That is correct. Carbon disulphide is a volatile liquid. The gas is also very irritant and if some of the liquid had been spilt accidentally and set on fire the victim would undoubtedly have inhaled some of the gas before he was overcome and would have sustained lung haemorrhages. Gentlemen, the autopsy showed that there were no lung haemorrhages.'

'So Schwartz was killed before the fire started?' said the district attorney.

'That again is perfectly correct,' replied the professor, with only a little irritation in his voice. 'But I'll come to that in a minute. I also found that the floor beneath the body was largely untouched by the fire, which again indicates that the fire was started after the body had been placed in position. In my opinion the fire was started to burn the body. The torches found by the fire chief were placed at strategic places in the lab and soaked with carbon disulphide. Then the body was dowsed in the liquid and a trail made to the door of the lab. The very inflammable liquid was then allowed to collect in the well of a bolt slot under the door, so that the door could be closed from outside and the small pool of liquid ignited by dropping a match into it. I found the remains of a match in the bolt slot. This would give the murderer time to get away before the fire got much of a hold.'

Veale and Tinning digested this in silence. 'Have you any clues as to how Schwartz was killed?' asked the district attorney eventually.

'Yes, I have,' answered Dr Heinrich. 'The victim was killed, in my opinion, by a blow or blows to the back of the head. In one place the wall of the laboratory shows some reddish patches. And I discovered some more in a small cupboard under the stairs. Gentlemen, those reddish stains were blood! I think that the victim was attacked in the laboratory and killed there. Then his body was stored in the cupboard under the stairs.'

'But that means,' said the sheriff, leaning forward in his chair, 'that the murder must have been committed some time before the fire started. And yet we know that Schwartz spoke to his wife on the phone only a short time before the explosion was heard.'

The scientist nodded in agreement. 'Perfectly correct,' he said with a sly smile. 'But then it is quite obvious, is it not, that the victim wasn't Schwartz?'

Veale looked nonplussed. 'But what about the identification?'

Dr Heinrich shook his head. 'I'm afraid that was a mistake.'

'But how can you explain all the people who saw the body and said it was Schwartz? The doctor and particularly the dentist, who identified it because of the missing tooth?'

'The body was quite unrecognisable because of the burning,' said the scientist quietly. 'And in this situation people were expecting it to be Schwartz. It was quite easy to make an error. If you remember I asked you to find out for me what Schwartz had for his last meal. You told me it was cucumber and beans. Well, the stomach of the dead man contained only some undigested meat – no trace of cucumber or beans. Then, one of the few parts of the body not destroyed by the fire was the right ear. Schwartz was known to have a mole on his right ear, but there was no trace of a mole on the ear of the body. The hair too wasn't the same. I asked you to get me one of Schwartz's hairbrushes, and comparing hairs from that with some from the body showed they were quite different.'

'What about the missing tooth in the right upper jaw?' asked District Attorney Tinning. 'Surely the dentist couldn't have been mistaken about that?'

'No, he couldn't,' agreed Dr Heinrich. 'But I examined the upper jaw of the body very carefully under a magnifying lens. And in my opinion the tooth was removed after death. Probably knocked out with a chisel, as there's still some of the root left in the gum.'

'So this means—', said Tinning slowly.

'Exactly,' broke in the scientist, 'it was a very carefully planned murder – probably by Schwartz himself.'

The sheriff had been sitting for some time in silence. Now he in turn nodded his head. 'I must admit it's all beginning to hang together. That break-in I told you about the other day at the Schwartz house. The only things stolen were photographs of Schwartz himself. If he'd set the thing up, plainly he'd forgotten to remove them, to make identification that much more difficult for us.'

'Yes and don't forget,' chimed in the district attorney, not wishing to be left out, 'the young man who saw the car speeding away, on the night of the fire, just after the explosion took place. He's convinced it was Schwartz's car. And since it's still missing it probably carried Schwartz.'

'And there's the evidence of Gonzales himself,' said Veale. 'If you remember he said he was going round with his dog on the night of the fire and the animal became very interested in the closet under the stairs. And Schwartz became angry and told Gonzales to take the animal away.'

'There's something else you may care to consider,' put in Dr Heinrich. 'I would say that this may have been planned by Schwartz for a long time. I'm a chemist myself and I can tell you that the factory was a fake. There's not even gas or water laid on. It would be impossible to manufacture artificial silk there. I think the whole place was set up to swindle gullible businessmen.'

'And when it didn't work out,' said the sheriff, 'and he ran into financial difficulties, possibly, and then had this breach-of-promise suit hanging round his neck, he decided to disappear. But to make the disappearance foolproof, he arranged a substitute.'

'Well,' said the district attorney decisively. 'We've two things to do now. Institute a search for Schwartz himself and try to get a line on who his unfortunate victim was.'

There came a deprecating cough from the scientist.

'Good Heavens!' exclaimed Tinning. 'Don't tell me you know who it is?'

The doctor smiled. 'Not quite. But I can give you a few clues. Examining the charred fragments of clothing from the corpse and debris from around the body under the microscope, I came to the conclusion that the man had been wearing a denim shirt, overalls and a jacket. Obviously not clothes that Schwartz himself would wear.

'Then I found some soap wrapped up in paper. Since the place had no running water Schwartz would not take soap into the laboratory with him. I also found some coffee similarly wrapped up and again it is doubtful if Schwartz would take coffee wrapped like that in with him. And finally I found a small sewing kit. Since

Schwartz had a wife at home who would do his sewing, what would he want with a sewing kit?

'All these clues indicate that the murdered man could have been some sort of itinerant worker, a man who moved from place to place and travelled light. I also found something else. There was some charred paper near the body which had probably been in the man's pockets. I managed to get enough of it together to discover that it had once been a small edition of the New Testament. There were also the remains of two pamphlets. One was "The Philosophy of Eternal Brotherhood" and the other was called "John, the Apostle". The man might thus have been an itinerant evangelist. There was also a fragment of paper with some handwriting on it. I've made a photograph of the script. If you could get the newspapers to print it, someone might recognise the writing.'

It was a long shot, but it paid off. An undertaker from Placerville, in northern California, saw the handwriting in the city newspapers and thought he recognised it. He drove to the coroner's office in San Francisco, where the body had been taken, and after viewing it said that it might well be that of his friend Gilbert Warren Barbe, who was a travelling missionary.

The undertaker sent for his wife and she recognised the coffee wrapped up in paper and the sewing kit as items she had given to Barbe.

The police had a talk with the undertaker and soon established how the missionary and the chemist came to meet. Barbe was fascinated by chemistry and answered an advertisement by Schwartz for an assistant chemist who should have small hands and feet.

The significance of this became clear when it was realised that Schwartz himself had small hands and feet. Gonzales also remembered a man coming to the factory to answer the advertisement, but he had never seen him again after that first sighting.

The search for the missing Schwartz had been going on since Dr Heinrich presented his report, and detectives scoured California, eventually extending the search to the whole of the United States of America and even overseas.

His background was thoroughly investigated and it was discovered that he was a conman who had had several aliases. His stories of exploits in the war were shown to be false. He had never flown in combat and his technical expertise, in an artillery battalion, had been restricted to that of company barber.

Since the case had received wide publicity in the press it wasn't long before the break came. An apartment house owner of Oakland, California, opened his daily newspaper one day and saw what he thought was a photograph of a boarder of his. It was a picture of Schwartz which the reporter had managed to borrow from an acquaintance of the chemist.

The proprietor went to the Berkeley police, since the towns of Oakland and Berkeley are very close, and saw Captain Clarence Lee. He told him that the boarder had moved in recently and paid a month's rent in advance. But the man avoided going out in the daytime, even taking his meals with the owner's family.

He had also had a distinctly nervous manner and would not talk about himself.

Captain Lee thought that it was worth while having a look at the mysterious stranger and quickly organised a squad of men. Arriving at the apartment house on 41st Street, he posted men at all the exits, then mounted the stairs, followed by the proprietor.

On the second floor he stopped outside the apartment indicated by the owner and banged on the door.

There was no reply from inside.

'Are you sure he's in?' enquired the captain.

'He never goes out.'

The captain banged again. 'Open the door. It's the police.'

Still there was no sound from the apartment.

'We'll have to break the door down,' said the captain, and he sent for his men to join him.

Soon there was a collection of heavy shoulders ready to charge the door.

But before they could begin, a shot rang out from inside.

And when finally the door was smashed open they found Schwartz lying across the bed, a revolver loosely gripped in his hand and blood trickling from a head wound. He was dead.

But ever the conman, a letter to his wife was found on the table beside the bed, in which he tried to justify his actions. He said that Barbe had come to him for a job and had then demanded money when Schwartz refused him. According to the chemist, a fight started and Barbe was killed accidentally. Schwartz then set the fire simply to cover his tracks.

I don't know whether his wife believed his story, but the police didn't.

9

The Secret Writing

'Can I borrow that ladder?' asked the young man.

The workman looked at him in surprise.

'My name', explained the speaker, 'is Henry Pasmore and I'm the representative of the Wolf's Head Oil Company in Southampton who rent the garage next door.'

'What of it?' asked the workman.

'I want to get into the property.'

'Haven't you got a key?'

'No,' said Pasmore patiently. 'The key's being held by the licensee of the pub you're working on. But he's out.'

'Can't you wait till he comes back?'

The young man breathed hard. 'I've only just taken up this appointment. The garage you see is also being used as a store room for oil. But it's been shut up and left unattended for two months and I'm anxious to get in and get on with the job of selling the oil.'

'All right, all right,' said the workman. 'No need to get on your high horse. What do you want the ladder for?'

'I thought if I could climb over the roof of the pub, it's only one storey, after all, I could get down into the alley beyond the gates and then into the garage.'

'Well,' said the workman doubtfully, 'it's up to you. You can borrow my ladder, but don't go and blame me if you fall and break your leg.'

'You can come with me and see that I don't, if you like.'

'You don't want much, do you?'

Nevertheless the reluctant labourer followed Pasmore over the low flat roof of the Royal Exchange public house. Taking the ladder with them they were able to climb down into the narrow alley behind the big double gates which fronted the garage property in Grove Street, Southampton.

It was a Thursday morning, 10 January 1929.

The two men were then confronted with another building which stood in the yard. It was two-storeyed and a ladder to the right of the door led up to a loft. But the folding door of the garage was padlocked.

'Have you got the key to that?' asked the workman.

'No, but we could wrench it off with a crowbar or something. I've been given permission to take whatever steps I feel necessary to get in and start selling oil again. The previous agent has cleared off and the company are anxious to restart business.'

The workman still looked doubtful. 'I suppose you know what you're doing. I'll go and get a crowbar, but I hope your company's going to pay me for the time spent trying to get you in.'

A short time later the padlock had been broken and the folding door – which required the concerted efforts of the two men – rolled back. Just inside on the left and facing inwards was a car, a four-seater maroon

Morris Oxford tourer, with its hood up. Drums of oil were stacked on the right, and between them and the vehicle a narrow passage had been left, which led to the rear.

The workman wrinkled his nose. 'What an awful smell! Has your oil gone off?'

'Lubricating oil doesn't go off that quickly in cold weather,' snapped Pasmore. He walked forward into the garage.

'My God!' he cried, after an interval. 'Come and look at this!'

The other man followed him in. Beyond the car was a line of crates almost up to the ceiling and beyond that, in a small bay between the piles of boxes, lay the remains of what had once been a man.

'His name was Vivian Messiter,' said Detective Inspector Chatfield of the Southampton police. 'He was fifty-five years old and the representative of the Wolf's Head Oil Company, which has its head office in London.'

Chatfield and two Scotland Yard detectives were standing outside the garage in Grove Street. It was the day following the discovery of the body. The man had suffered severe head injuries, which could not be attributed to a fall, nor could they have been self-inflicted; it was obviously a murder. The Chief Constable of Southampton had therefore called in Scotland Yard the same day and Chief Detective Inspector Prothero and his assistant, Detective Sergeant Young, had caught a night train from London. After a few hours snatched sleep they accompanied the Southampton detective to the garage.

'The body was in a terrible state,' continued Chatfield. 'The face black and unrecognisable and part of it eaten away, presumably by rats.' He shuddered as he remembered how he had to examine the body before it was taken away for postmortem examination.

'How was it identified?' asked Chief Inspector Prothero quickly, in the cultured voice which had led him to being called 'Gentleman John' by his colleagues.

The inspector drew a hand across his face. 'By the clothes and a latch key found in his pocket. The identification was made by Messiter's landlord, Mr Parrott, who reported him missing some weeks ago.'

'What sort of a chap was this Messiter?' enquired John Prothero.

Chatfield scratched his chin. 'Very quiet, according to Mrs Parrott. Spoke with an American accent, though he was apparently an Englishman. But he'd spent a lot of time out there. Walked with a bit of a limp as he'd been shot through the thigh in the war.'

'A man of regular habits?' prompted the chief inspector.

'Apparently so. Had his breakfast at eight o'clock every morning and went to work, returning about three or four o'clock in the afternoon to write letters. Then he went out to dinner each night at six thirty and returned not later than half past eight or nine. About ten weeks ago – that would be Tuesday, the 30th of October, last year – he had his breakfast half an hour earlier as he said he had an appointment in town. He

went out after breakfast and didn't return and neithe'
of the Parrotts had seen him since.'

The three men turned into the entrance of the garage
The Morris Oxford had been wheeled out and v
standing in the yard.

Inspector Chatfield stopped by the car. 'We found a
couple of books on the front seat, near the steering
wheel. An exercise book and an account book.'

'Where are they?'

'Locked up in the safe in the Chief Constable's Office
at Bargate Police Station.'

Prothero nodded his head.

'We also found a grey overcoat, presumably belonging to the deceased. He was wearing a brown overall
when he was found and had possibly been working on
the car or with the oil at the time of his death.'

After a brief examination of the vehicle, the three
men entered the white-walled garage, which still had
the smell of decomposition and decay clinging to it,
mixed with the cloying smell of the oil.

'We didn't find any money or valuables on the body,'
continued Chatfield, 'and though we did find the swivel
ring of a gold watch on the floor, the watch itself seems
to be missing.'

'It sounds as if robbery could be the motive,' said
the chief inspector. He turned to the Southampton
detective with a smile. 'You've done a good job, inspector, but since I'm taking over I'd like to start out
afresh.' As Prothero began issuing his instructions, Sergeant Young made notes. 'I'd like a thorough search
of the premises. And everything, but everything,

catalogued. I want to know where every matchstick, scrap of paper and cigarette butt has been found.'

Chatfield nodded and led the way to where the body d been discovered. In the little alcove where it had lain the smell was strong. Although the body had gone, pools of dried blood still marked the concrete floor and there were even blood splashes on the boxes and crates circling the area.

The chief inspector looked round carefully. 'From the height of the blood, I would say the man was struck down while he was leaning over. Has the pathologist any idea of the weapon?'

'Dr Seager Thomas thinks the man might have been shot.'

'Better have a good look round for bullets, then.'

'Will you be going to the postmortem, sir?' enquired Chatfield, and John Prothero said that he would.

Dr Seager Thomas was a tall man with glasses. As he stripped off his rubber gloves and washed his hands under the running tap after the examination he said, 'As you saw there were three separate injuries to the head; one behind the right ear at the back, another over the right ear and the third to the frontal bone centred at about the inner corner of the left eye. Each one caused extensive damage to the bones of the skull and they were the undoubted cause of death.'

'Can you tell what caused them, doctor?'

'It's very difficult. As you saw, most of the soft tissue in the head has gone, but one of the wounds might have been a bullet wound.'

The pathologist was also able to confirm that the

body must have lain where it was found for at least two months, and a date near the end of October might be a possible time of death.

'If I could make a suggestion?' asked Dr Seager Thomas. 'I think the services of Sir Bernard Spilsbury, if they can be obtained, would be most helpful.'

The next day a constable searching the garage found a hammer behind some oil drums near one of the side walls. It was afterwards described as a continental-pattern riveting hammer, with a head having one square end and coming to a point at the other. Both the head and the shaft were stained with what looked like blood.

The hammer was passed on to Sir Bernard Spilsbury, who found an eyebrow hair which matched those of Vivian Messiter on the metal head. The stains on the shaft and head were subsequently shown to be human blood by Dr Roche Lynch, Senior Official Analyst to the Home Office. Sir Bernard also conducted another autopsy and gave it as his opinion that all the blows to the head could have been caused by the hammer.

At the Bargate Police Station Prothero and Young examined the two books which had been found on the front seat of Messiter's car.

One was an ordinary exercise book and the other a duplicate book with pages in pairs, which were meant to have carbon paper between them.

The chief inspector handled the exercise book carefully, touching it only at the edges. 'We'll have to get Inspector Battley down from the Yard to have a look for fingerprints.'

Prothero passed the book over to Young. 'You'll notice there appears to be a page missing.'

The sergeant nodded his head. 'Yes, but it's not the last page in the book with writing on it. The last one says: "October 30, 1928, Received from Wolf's Head Oil Company, commission on order, S. Gover. 5 gallons heavy, six pence – 2s 6d." And it's signed H. F. Galton. Am I right in thinking, sir, that this H. Galton signed for a commission of sixpence per gallon obtained by selling oil for Messiter?'

'Looks like it. But notice the date. According to the Parrotts, the 30th of October was the last day they saw him alive. We'll have to try and trace this Galton, who presumably was an agent working for Messiter.'

They turned their attention to the duplicate book.

'There's several top copies torn out here,' commented John Prothero, 'as you might expect from a duplicate book. But some of the bottom pages have been removed as well.' He passed the book over to Young. 'Why would anyone do that?'

'Because both sets of pages contained incriminating material?'

The chief inspector nodded. 'On the other hand, Messiter might have torn out those pages himself. We shall have to check at the garage and his lodgings to see if he's thrown them away.'

'There are some carbon sheets tucked in the back here, sir.'

'Are there? Well, don't handle them. I'll get James O'Brien from the Photographic Department down here to have a look at them. He might be able to get some impressions from them.'

The two detectives went to Carlton Road in Southampton, where Messiter had lodged. Mr Parrott, who was an ex-policeman, had carefully kept all the murdered man's papers. Prothero and Young first made a meticulous search of the room the man had used, but they found no missing duplicate pages or anything else of interest.

The papers however were more promising. The Scotland Yard men found that the oil man had put an advert in the *Southern Daily Echo*, the local newspaper, asking for men with local knowledge to sell oil on commission. It had been answered by two correspondents, Harold Galton and a W. F. Thomas, and Messiter, careful man that he was, had kept both letters with their addresses.

Prothero and Young went to see Galton.

He lived in Oakley Road and worked for the Southern Railway. He agreed that he had answered the advert on the 23rd of October.

'And you went to the garage in Grove Street?' asked the chief inspector.

'No, sir. I never went there at all. Mr Messiter came here to see me.'

'He actually called here?'

'Yes, sir. Twice. No, three times it was because he called once when I was out and came again the same day.'

'What day was that?'

Galton looked uncomfortable. 'I'm afraid I've forgotten the date.'

'All right. Let's turn to the last time you saw him and received commission. That would be on Tuesday the 30th of October?'

The railway man again looked embarrassed. 'No, sir, that was Monday night, the 29th. Mr Messiter dated it the day after because that was when the oil was going to be delivered.'

'And you didn't go to the garage on the morning of 30th?'

'I've never been to the garage at all, sir. I don't even know where it is.'

'Do you believe him, sir?' asked Sergeant Young as they came away from the house.

'I don't know. We'll see if he has an alibi. In the meantime we'll go and see Mr Thomas.'

But Thomas was not at home. In fact he had not been at the address given in his letter, Cranbury Avenue, since early in November. His landlady, Mrs Horne, said he had arrived with his wife, a young blonde lady, on the 20th of October. The rent was fifteen shillings a week, in advance, and Thomas paid ten shillings down and a further five shillings the same evening. He said that he was a motor engineer. The next payment became due on the 27th of October, but Thomas put it off until the following Tuesday, the 30th, when he paid the full amount at six in the evening. He and his wife departed on the following Saturday, leaving a forwarding address in the Chiswick Road in London.

Further evidence linking Thomas with Messiter turned up shortly after. Two pieces of paper were discovered in the garage. One, screwed up into a ball and oil stained, was found on the floor in the sawdust behind a couple of drums. The writing was difficult to make out, but it looked like an order for 35 or 36 gallons of oil and the signature bore a resemblance to that of Thomas. This seemed to be confirmed when the other side turned out to be a receipt for rent money, signed by Mrs Horne's son.

The other was found in the back room of the garage in a small drawer. When unrolled it carried the message 'Mr W. F. Thomas, I shall be at Grove Street, at 10 a.m. but not noon', and it was signed 'V. Messiter'.

'This definitely puts Thomas in the garage at some time or other,' remarked Chief Inspector Prothero. He, Sergeant Young and Inspector Chatfield were discussing the case in the office at Bargate Police Station that Prothero had taken over for his headquarters.

'Now I want you, inspector,' continued Prothero, 'to circulate these two names, Galton and Thomas, around other police forces. I've got a feeling about this case. It could well be that one or other of them was on some sort of fiddle. Claiming commission for oil which he hadn't sold. Messiter found out and was killed. And I also have a suspicion that one of them might have a record.'

'What about the hammer, sir?' asked Chatfield. 'Shall I circulate a description of that?'

'Yes, in the newspapers, particularly the local ones.

Get them to publish a photograph of it. Somebody might recognise it as having been stolen from them.'

There was soon a response to this. A Mr Henry Marsh who lived in Grosvenor Square, Southampton, called at his local police station to say that he thought it was his hammer. He had filed down the end of his and it looked identical to the one in the photograph. After examining the hammer he said that it was indeed his because he recognised a burn mark he had made when fitting a new shaft. Marsh was employed at the Morris Motor Works in Southampton and used the tool in his work. One day near the end of October his foreman brought a man to see him who said he was a motor engineer and wanted to borrow a hammer to do some repairs on his car. Marsh lent the man his hammer and never saw it again.

This could have been vital evidence, but unfortunately Marsh could not give a very clear description of the man, except to say that he had a small scar on his forehead. The police description of the man they wanted to interview in connection with the murder was thus reported in the newspapers under the heading 'the man with the scar'.

Better news came from the Wiltshire police. On the 15th of January, John Prothero received a message that the Wiltshire police were also looking for a man named Thomas. It was obviously the same person since he had signed himself W. F. Thomas with an address in Cranbury Avenue, Southampton, when he had applied for a job with a building contractor who lived at Downton, seven or eight miles south of Salisbury. He had begun the job, first as a motor mechanic and then as a driver, on the 3rd of November – the date Thomas left his lodgings in Southampton – and left on the 21st of December. And when he went, wage packets containing over £130 of his employer's money disappeared as well.

This looked like the first positive lead to the murderer, since Galton had an alibi for all day Tuesday the 30th of October, had no scar on his forehead and could not be associated any further with Messiter.

Prothero and Young immediately went to Downton. They found the house where Thomas and his wife had lodged and searched the room they had occupied. Sergent Young looked inside a vase standing on the mantelpiece.

'There's something here,' he said and up-ended the ornament. Out fell a folded piece of paper. 'It's a blank docket from an order book. The heading is "Auto and Radio Services", with an address in London Road, Manchester.'

'You could check with the firm, when we get back, and see if they've ever had a Thomas working for them. Or better still ring the police in Manchester and see if they've heard of a Thomas.'

But they hadn't. Sergeant Young explained the nature of the investigation and mentioned a possible connection with 'Auto and Radio Services'. The officer at the other end promised to make enquiries.

A while later Young received a return telephone call. 'I've got something here you may be interested in,' said the Manchester policeman. 'In connection with "Auto

and Radio Services", we are looking for a man called
Podmore, William Henry Podmore, who used to work
there and is wanted for the theft of a motor car from
them.'

Sergeant Young found that Podmore had a long
police record. He obtained the file and showed it to his
superior.

'Do you think he's our man, sir?'

'I think it's a strong possibility. Show Podmore's
picture to the landlady at Cranbury Avenue. See if she
recognises it.'

Both Mrs Horne and her son recognised the photograph as that of W. F. Thomas.

Podmore was a native of Staffordshire, where he was
well known to the police. He was married, but had left
his wife and was living with a blonde lady called Lil
who bore a strong resemblance to the young woman
who had been with Thomas in Southampton and
Downton.

Chief Inspector Prothero got in touch with the Staffordshire police and Detective Inspector Diggle of that
force made enquiries at Podmore's home in Hanley.
He found that Podmore had stayed there over Christmas, but had left in the New Year with Lil to take up
a position as a garage hand at the Stonebridge Hotel,
Meriden, near Birmingham.

The proprietor of the hotel confirmed that Podmore
– for some unknown reason he then went under his
own name – and 'Mrs Podmore' had arrived on the
5th of January. Six days later, when reports of the
Southampton murder appeared in the newspapers, he

appeared to panic. He told his employer that he and his wife were leaving and asked for his wages. The proprietor said he could have them when the stocks were checked – Podmore was responsible for the filling station at the hotel – but he could not wait and left without his wages.

Inspector Diggle eventually traced 'Lil' to her home in Stoke-on-Trent, where she had gone after she and Podmore parted when they left the Stonebridge Hotel. She readily admitted to living with him in Southampton, Downton and Meriden, and confirmed that he had seemed upset when he saw accounts of the murder in the newspapers. She also thought he had gone to London, and mentioned the Leicester Hotel in Vauxhall Bridge Road, where they had stayed previously.

When this was reported to Chief Inspector Prothero in Southampton he got in touch with Scotland Yard and Detective Inspector Simmonds and a police sergeant went to the Leicester Hotel. They found Podmore sitting up in bed reading a newspaper. He had a small scar on his forehead.

After identifying themselves the police told Podmore they were arresting him. 'I know what you want me for,' said the man, 'but I can explain everything. In fact my reason for coming to London was to go to Scotland Yard. I telephoned them last night, but couldn't get through.'

He was taken to the Gerald Road Police Station and from there to Southampton, where he was handed over to the chief inspector. He then made a statement.

It was obvious that he'd had plenty of time to concoct a story to account for the evidence he must have guessed the police possessed. He admitted that he'd assumed the name of Thomas, because the police in Manchester were looking for him under the name of Podmore, and confessed to having met Messiter. He even admitted being at the garage on the day the oil man was last seen alive, but said he'd left Messiter in the company of another man, called 'Maxton' or 'Baxton', and he gave a detailed description of him.

'He's very clever,' remarked John Prothero, when Podmore's statement had been taken. 'He knows we've very little to tie him in with Messiter. We don't even have decent evidence of a motive.'

'What about those carbon sheets we found in the duplicate book?' asked Sergeant Young.

The police had been able to make out some names and addresses left on the carbons. There were traces of a bill to Cromer and Bartlet, 25 Bold Street, Southampton. But after much searching the two detectives failed to find a Bold Street in Southampton. They did find a Bold Street, however, near to where Podmore used to live, in Stoke-on-Trent. There were also signs of another bill to a man called Baskerfield. No trace of anyone of that name could be found in Southampton, but again there was a man called Baskeyfield whom Podmore had known in the Potteries. Faint marks of an account to a Clayton Farm, which didn't exist near Southampton, but was known in Staffordshire, were also found.

'The bills which are missing,' continued Young, 'may

seem like coincidences, but to me they point to the fact that Podmore was systematically inventing people to whom he had sold oil in order to collect the commission. Messiter found out he was being defrauded and Podmore killed him.'

'I agree,' said the chief inspector. 'If we can prove that he wrote them. But we can't. And a jury will need more than coincidences.'

The exercise book containing the receipt made out to Galton and the duplicate book were taken out of the chief constable's safe and shown to the jury at the inquest, together with the carbon paper with the imprints of the false names and addresses. In those days the inquest often preceded committal proceedings and took the form of a mini-trial. But the evidence against Podmore was too weak to convince the jury, who brought in a verdict of 'murder by person or persons unknown'.

After the inquest, when the books were being returned to the safe, John Prothero picked up the exercise book and flicking through the pages came to the one with Galton's receipt on it. He gazed at it for a while, then carried it to the window and held it so that the light fell obliquely across the page. Then he turned to his companions and a slow smile appeared on his face.

'This time I think we've got him.' He handed the book to Sergeant Young. 'See if you can make out the impression of any letters on that receipt.'

Young peered at it for some time. 'I think I can

make out the words "Cromer and Bartlet" and then "five galls".'

'Good. It's obviously the impression of an entry made on the previous page. The one that has been torn out. See if you can see the signature.'

Sergeant Young was silent for some time, then he read out haltingly, 'W. F. T.'

'Exactly. It's Thomas's. And if I'm not mistaken the writing will correspond to that on the letter Podmore, alias Thomas, sent to Messiter. We'll be able to confirm it, I believe, by having light from a strong lamp thrown across the page and getting it photographed by O'Brien. I think we'll find that this is one of the false transactions Podmore worked on Messiter. And it's the only one which carries his signature. But the important thing is that it has been torn out. If the murder had not been committed by Podmore, the murderer would have no need to destroy evidence connecting Podmore with Messiter. Only if Podmore was himself the murderer would there be any point in doing that. And by taking that action he's damned himself.'

Although the trial did not take place for another year – Podmore first served six months for the theft at Manchester and a further six months for the offence at Downton – the jury agreed with the chief inspector. Podmore was convicted of murder at the Hampshire Assizes, held at Winchester before Lord Hewart, in March 1930, and after his appeal had been dismissed, hanged in April of the same year.

10

The Judas Window

Officer. Can you help me?'

The burly Berlin policeman looked up at the man sitting on the box seat of the cart and holding the horse's reins.

'I can't get into my flat,' said the man. He was about fifty years of age, short in stature and had on a greasy cap and an old jacket with a muffler round his neck.

'Lost your key?' queried the policeman suspiciously. 'Is that it?'

The man on the cart shook his head. 'The door's bolted on the inside.'

'Wife locked you out, then?'

'No, no.' The carter shook his head again impatiently. 'You don't understand. I've knocked and knocked. But there's no sound.'

'So, she's not answering. Have you had a row?'

The small workman got down from his cart and held the horse by the bridle. He now looked up at the burly policeman. 'You still don't understand do you? There's not a sound from inside my home. And I've got five children in there!'

The policeman suddenly became businesslike. 'Get someone to look after your horse and cart and show me where you live.'

The workman, whose named turned out to be Conrad, lived not far away in a large tenement block near the city centre. The year was 1881 and in those days tenements could be very forbidding buildings. The two men climbed the stone stairs, past the peeling plaster walls, to the fourth floor, picking their way around the clutter of rubbish which littered the stairs and passageways. There were already curious neighbours congregating in the corridor when they arrived at Conrad's front door.

The burly policeman banged on the door in the ill-lit passage and shouted fruitlessly for some time, then he turned to the small man by his side.

'I can't break in without permission from the landlord and as this might be a serious matter we'd better go to the police station and make a report.'

Sometime later Conrad, accompanied by a detective of the Berlin police, a carpenter and the owner of the building, returned to the door of the flat.

'I don't want any evidence destroyed if it can be avoided,' said the detective to the carpenter. 'Can you get the door open without wrecking the lock?'

'I don't know about that.' The carpenter looked again at the flimsy woodwork. 'It's not very substantial, though. I might be able to lever it off the hinges.'

This he eventually managed to do and when he had forced it back enough for the men to squeeze through they discovered that the door had indeed been bolted on the inside.

But an even more startling and terrible discovery

was awaiting them in the room which served as living accommodation for the Conrad family.

There, hanging from a hook in the wall, was the emaciated body of Conrad's wife. A rope around her neck, which had almost disappeared into the thin flesh and caused her face to turn purple, told its own story. But there was no sign of the five children.

Then, in the next room, in a small closet which served as a wardrobe, five pitiful bodies were discovered. Like their mother they were no more than skin and bone and each had been hung, with a rope round its neck, from hooks in the wall.

Conrad collapsed on to a chair in the living room.

Immediately a doctor and an examining magistrate, who would be in charge of the case, were summoned.

Herr Hollman, the magistrate, arrived with the doctor who carefully examined the bodies which had been taken down from the hooks in the walls, while Conrad was taken off to the police station to make a statement.

'What do you think?' Hollman asked the doctor.

The medical man looked up from his examination of the body of Frau Conrad. 'It certainly looks like strangulation, but I'll be able to tell better after the autopsy.'

The magistrate scratched his head. 'What do you think happened here?'

The doctor stood up. 'I think there's little doubt, don't you? The poor woman strangled her five children, then strung herself up. A tragic case. By the looks of her and the children they were half-starved.

Presumably, short of money and food, she decided to end it all for herself and her family. Unfortunately a situation which is not unknown these days in this great city of ours.'

'Yes, indeed,' agreed Hollman. 'But did you notice the husband? He looked poorly dressed, but he didn't appear to be half-starved like his family.'

'Well, that's true – but there cannot be any question, can there? The door was bolted on the inside, so nobody could have entered from the outside. The windows are too high for anyone to climb up and enter that way. And the only other way is down the chimney.' The doctor allowed himself a slight smile. 'And I think we can eliminate that since the chimneys in these apartments are too narrow to climb down.'

The magistrate nodded in agreement. 'Yes, the inescapable conclusion seems to be that the poor lady must have murdered her children and then taken her own life. But somehow it just doesn't sound right to me.'

'Why ever not?'

'Does it sound right to you? A woman in despair might well kill herself, but would she kill all her children as well?'

'People who commit suicide are usually in what we consider an abnormal state of mind,' said the doctor in a judicious voice. 'And in that state who can tell what people will do?'

'I'm still not happy about it,' muttered the magistrate.

He had Conrad brought to his office and interviewed him. The little man's explanation of the tragedy was that his wife had been worried over money. But the magistrate was still not convinced that he had the true story and he therefore asked the police to interview neighbours and find out what sort of man this Conrad was and what his relations were with his wife.

The reports soon began coming in. Frau Conrad had seemed normal to her neighbours, albeit in despair at times with the lack of money coming in, but that was a condition she shared with many of her fellow tenement-dwellers. But in no way had she struck the women who knew her as a person likely to kill her children and then commit suicide.

On the other hand their opinion of the husband was much less favourable. He was regarded as lazy. He was often away from home for long periods and at these times his wife and family were desperately short of money. Nevertheless he thought of himself as an intellectual, far above the mental standard of his neighbours.

Hollman studied these reports then called the chief of detectives to his office. 'I'd like this man Conrad followed,' he said. 'I want to know where he goes and whom he meets.'

A few days later the detective chief reported back. 'We've come up with something,' he said, taking the chair offered him by the magistrate. 'We've followed Conrad and found that he has a girlfriend.'

'Ah,' said Herr Hollman sitting back in his chair. 'Tell me about her.'

'We haven't found out a great deal yet, but we know

that she's a servant in a big house and she's some thirty years younger than him.'

'It's the old story, isn't it?' said the magistrate. 'An older man falls for a young girl. If he's poor, like Conrad, the money he spends on her will come out of the family budget. His family will go short.'

'Yes, sir. I understand that he's spent quite a lot of money on her in the past.'

'We'll have Conrad in again, see if we can get anything out of him.'

But again Hollman had a fruitless interview with the carter. While the man admitted he had a girlfriend – 'It's not against the law is it?' – he steadfastly refused to agree that he had spent money on her. And he challenged the magistrate to prove that he had anything to do with his wife's death. 'Your policeman can prove that I couldn't get into the flat. He couldn't get in himself!'

After the interview the chief of detectives and the magistrate discussed the situation.

'We've nothing to go on, sir,' said the detective chief. 'Unless we can get him or his girlfriend to admit that she put pressure on him, there's no motive for him to kill his wife. Apart from the fact that I can't see how he did it anyway – if he did.'

The magistrate nodded, but said nothing.

'If you don't mind me saying so, sir,' continued the detective, 'perhaps we ought to take the simplest explanation as the right one. Since no one could possibly have got into that room after the bolt was secured on

the inside, Frau Conrad must indeed have killed all her children and then committed suicide herself.'

Herr Hollman pursed his lips. 'I simply can't get out of my head the impression that that's what we are supposed to think.'

'That Conrad's being clever? I can't see it myself. After all he's only a workman. Drives a horse and cart for a living. If this was a murder it was a sophisticated one. Done very cleverly. That doesn't sound like Conrad to me, does it to you?'

'No, it doesn't,' admitted the magistrate.

'Look, can I make a suggestion? Let me and my detectives go to the flat when Conrad's not there and have a final search to see if we can find anything incriminating. If this girlfriend of his has been putting pressure on him she might have written him letters. If we can find any we'll at least have a lever we can use on him. And he might then admit to something. But if we don't find anything, will you agree to drop the case?'

'I suppose you're right,' said Hollman. 'I tell you what. I'll come with you. Just you and I. We'll search the apartment together.'

And so a few days later the two men, having obtained keys from the owner of the property, climbed the steep narrow steps one afternoon when they knew Conrad would be away on a long carting job. The upper parts of the wall had once been white but the whitewash had long since turned a dingy grey and large portions of the plaster had fallen away exposing the bricks. The two men let themselves into the apartment.

Looking around, the magistrate realised that their

search would not take them long. There was hardly any furniture in the flat. In the main room which also served as the kitchen there was a table, a few rickety chairs and a large cupboard on the wall which had contained the family's small store of food and cooking utensils. Above one of the better chairs, which stood by the stove, was a crudely made shelf of books.

'One member of the family at least could read,' remarked Hollman pointing to the books.

'That's Conrad himself,' replied the detective. 'The neighbours say he boasts that he's a great reader.'

The magistrate nodded. 'Well, books are a good place to secretly store letters. You have a look through the cupboard, I'll see if there is anything concealed in these books.'

The detective chief made a careful search of the cupboard on the wall without finding anything useful and then, seeing that the magistrate seemed to be engrossed in the books, he began a search of the rest of the room. When he had finished this he went into the bedroom which the whole family had shared.

An hour later he returned to the living room. Hollman was now sitting on the chair by the stove, a pile of books on the floor beside him and a book open on his knees.

'Nothing doing, I'm afraid, sir.'

'Eh?' the magistrate looked up, somewhat startled, from the book he was reading.

'There's absolutely nothing in the bedroom, or in this room come to that, that sheds any light on the mystery – if mystery it is.'

'Ah, yes,' said Hollman vaguely, 'I'm sure you're right.'

'Have you found anything?' asked the detective rather pointedly.

'I'm not sure,' replied the magistrate in an uncertain voice.

The chief of detectives heaved a sigh. 'Did you want to continue here?'

At last Herr Hollman looked up. 'I don't think there's any more that you can do. You get off if you want to, I'll return the keys.'

'Are you sure you don't mind?' asked the detective, anxious to be off now that he was convinced they had come to the end of a fruitless task. If the magistrate wanted to sit by the stove and read somebody else's books, that was up to him. But he had work to do.

'Yes, you go,' said Hollman. 'Come and see me in my office in the morning, would you?'

The following morning the detective chief went to the magistrate's office and found Hollman still looking slightly preoccupied, and gazing down at the desk in front of him. The detective felt he ought to open the conversation.

'Are we agreed then, sir, that we'll accept the most likely explanation of the deaths as an unfortunate lapse by Frau Conrad, followed by her suicide?'

'By no means,' said the magistrate looking up. 'Conrad definitely murdered his wife and children. The difficulty is going to be proving it.'

The detective gaped. 'But how . . . ?' he spluttered.

Herr Hollman got to his feet. 'Tell you about it later.

At the moment we've got one chance and one chance only of bringing this murder home to Conrad and that is to get him to confess. Come along!'

Together the two men made their way to the tenement where Conrad had his poor home. The detective said nothing, but he was thinking that the magistrate seemed to have an obsession about this case, expecting Conrad to confess when they had no more evidence against him now than they had when they started.

Up the narrow stone stairs they clattered again to the fourth floor. Herr Hollman knocked on Conrad's door and it was opened by the carter himself.

'Can we come in?' asked the magistrate pushing forward so that the little man was forced to let them in.

Hollman and the policeman moved into the centre of the small room. There, by the stove, was a chair and by the side of that, on the floor, an open book. The detective thought to himself that Conrad must have been in the same position, just before they knocked, that the magistrate had been in the last time he had seen him in the flat.

'Herr Conrad,' said Hollman sombrely. 'We're going to take you down to headquarters and charge you with the murder of your wife and five children!'

The detective looked at the magistrate in alarm. Had the man taken leave of his senses? But Hollman looked quite calm.

'Get your cap and then we'll go,' he told the small man.

The three men went out into the passage. 'Make

sure you lock your door behind you,' Hollman said to Conrad.

The carter took a key from his pocket and carefully locked the recently repaired door.

The magistrate turned to the chief of detectives. 'Will you take Herr Conrad down to the next floor and wait for me there?'

The detective shot Hollman a puzzled glance and noticed a somewhat anxious look on the magistrate's face. But he decided that since he had come this far in the charade he might as well go on with it. He took the prisoner by the arm. 'Come along, Herr Conrad.' And together the policeman and the carter walked down the stone stairs to the floor below.

A few minutes later they were joined by Herr Hollman. But this time there was a smile on his face as he came down the stairs to meet them.

'Can we now go back up again?' he asked.

Conrad and the detective exchanged a glance, but they both followed him back up the stairs without comment.

When they reached Conrad's door again Hollman leaned nonchalantly on the wall. 'We'll just go back inside, please, Herr Conrad.'

A puzzled look appeared on the small man's face. 'What is this?'

'If you please, Herr Conrad.'

The carter shrugged his shoulders, then reached into his pocket and withdrew the key. He turned it in the lock and pushed the door.

The door refused to budge.

The detective stepped forward. 'Perhaps it's stuck. Here, let me try.' He turned the key himself and pushed, but the door remained stubbornly shut. He put his shoulder against it, but it still remained immovable. He stepped backwards preparing to make a charge against the door. But the magistrate's voice stopped him.

'It won't open, will it, Herr Conrad?' asked Hollman calmly. 'Because it's bolted from the inside!'

He was still leaning against the wall, looking down at the small man.

Conrad gazed up at him. 'You know, don't you?' he wailed.

The magistrate nodded slowly in reply.

Large tears suddenly formed in the carter's eyes and ran down his cheeks. 'I couldn't help it! She said she wouldn't see me again unless I agreed to marry her!'

'So you killed six people. Your wife and your own small children!'

'I'm in love with her! She means everything in the world to me!'

The man buried his face in his hands and began to sob uncontrollably. Hollman placed his hand on the small man's shoulder and gently steered him towards the stairs.

Some hours later, when Conrad had made his confession at the police station and it had all been taken down and properly signed, the chief of detectives and the magistrate went back to the flat.

Once again they had to wait until the door was taken

off its hinges for them to enter and once again the door was discovered to be bolted on the inside.

'It was very nearly the perfect crime,' said Hollman when the two men had gained admittance and seated themselves as comfortably as they could on either side of the stove.

'After Conrad had murdered his wife and children he went out and closed the door behind him. But previously he had bored a small hole just above the bolt and threaded through a thin piece of twisted horse hair. One end was attached to the handle of the bolt so that by pulling from outside he could draw the bolt home. He had made sure, of course, before he started that the bolt was well greased and would draw easily. When the bolt was finally home all he had to do was to jerk the twisted hair and most if it would come through the hole and he could remove it. The small hole remaining in the door he filled from the outside with putty stained to look the same colour as the door itself. He counted on the small piece of horse hair still remaining on the bolt on the inside not being noticed when the door was forced open.'

'That's incredible!' said the detective chief jumping up and going over to examine the door. 'And you used the same trick on him today?'

'Yes. I had to use a piece of wire instead. I put it in place yesterday when we were in the flat, and I was worried that he might have noticed it when he came home last night, but he obviously didn't. But of course he guessed what I had done when he found the door bolted from the inside this morning. And discovering that his secret method had been exposed tipped him over the edge into a confession, as I hoped it would.'

'Amazing,' murmured the chief. 'But I'll tell you what is more amazing to me and that is that Conrad managed to figure out such a method himself.'

'Of course he didn't,' replied the magistrate. 'And to be perfectly honest I didn't either. This is one of the most incredible things about this case. Look at that shelf of books over there.' The detective looked up at the crude piece of wood fixed to the wall and the row of shabby books standing upon it. 'Everyone assumed', continued Hollman, 'that Conrad was a bit of an intellectual because he read books. But those are all trashy novels, as I discovered yesterday. But one of them seemed to fall open at a certain place when I took it down. I looked for concealed letters, but didn't find any. Then I had a closer look at the book.'

Here he stood up and running his finger along the book spines came to a halt at one, pulled it out and handed it to the detective.

'*Nena Sahib* by John Ratcliffe,' read the chief. 'It's a translation of an English book?'

'That's right. It's actually a detective story, about an Indian nobleman who is found dead in a room in London, which is bolted on the inside! Everyone suspects suicide until an English detective discovers a small hole in the door near the bolt through which a thin wire could be placed to draw the bolt home from the outside. Though I must say that Conrad improved on the book because he used horse hair instead, which is much less noticeable.'

Conrad was eventually tried, convicted and hanged. The case is one of the very few where life seems to follow art.

Bibliography

Belin, Jean, *My Work At The Sûreté* (Geo. G. Harrap, 1950)

Bennett, Benjamin, *Murder Will Speak* (Howard Timmins, 1962)

Block, Eugene L., *The Chemist of Crime* (Cassell, 1959)

Bolitho, William, *Murder For Profit* (Jonathan Cape, 1933)

Browne, Douglas G. and Tullett, E. V., *Bernard Spilsbury* (Geo. G. Harrap, 1951)

Douthwaite, L. C., *Mass Murder* (John Long, 1928)
The Royal Canadian Mounted Police (Blackie and Son, 1939)

Fletcher Moulton, H. and Lloyd Woodland, W., *The Trial of William Henry Podmore* (Geoffrey Bles, 1931)

Godwin, John, *Killers In Paradise* (Herbert Jenkins, 1962)

Goodman, Jonathan, *The Country House Murders* (Allison and Busby, 1987)

Grex, Leo, *Detection Stranger Than Fiction* (Ravette, 1985)
Mystery Stranger Than Fiction (St Martin's Press, 1979)

Gribble, Leonard, *Adventures In Murder* (John Long, 1954)
Famous Detective Feats (Arthur Barker, 1971)

Famous Feats of Detection & Deduction (Geo. G. Harrap, 1933)

Famous Manhunts (John Long, 1953)

Grierson, Francis, *Famous French Crimes* (Frederick Muller, 1959)

Heppenstall, Rayner, *Bluebeard and After* (Peter Owen, 1972)

Huson, Richard, *Sixty Famous Trials* (Daily Express Publication)

Irving, H. B., *Studies of French Criminals* (William Heinemann, 1901)

Lindsay, Philip, *The Mainspring of Murder* (John Long, 1958)

Lloyd Woodland, W., *Assize Pageant* (Geo. G. Harrap, 1952)

Mackenzie, F. A., *Landru* (Geoffrey Bles, 1928)

Malcolm, M. J., *Murder in the Yukon* (Western Producer Prairie Books, 1982)

Montgomery Hyde, H., *United In Crime* (William Heinemann, 1955)

Sharpe, Alan, *Crimes That Shocked Australia* (Atrand, 1987)

Singer, Kurt, *My Strangest Case* (W. H. Allen, 1957)

Thorwald, Jurgen, *Crime and Science* (Harcourt, Brace and World, 1967)

Wilkins, Philip A., *Behind The French CID* (Hutchinson, 1941)

Wilson, Colin, *The Mammoth Book of True Crime* (Robinson Publishing, 1988)

Written In Blood (Equation, 1989)

Wren, Lassiter, *Masterstrokes Of Crime Detection* (Double-day, Doran and Company, 1929)

Young, Hugh, *My Forty Years At The Yard* (W. H. Allen, 1955)

The files of the *Daily Klondike Nugget, Edmonton Journal, Southern Daily Echo, Sydney Morning Herald, The Times, Vancouver Daily News-Advertiser.*

THE CONFESSIONS OF HENRY LEE LUCAS

Mike Cox

IN THE BACKWOODS OF VIRGINIA, HE WAS BORN TO KILL

Henry Lee Lucas was schooled in sexual deviance and cruelty by an abusive mother. He soon derived twisted pleasure from torturing farm animals, then savagely slaying them. At the age of 24, his lust for killing led him to take his first human life . . . his mother's. In and out of prison until he was 33, this quiet, polite, one-eyed drifter would keep on murdering, and leave in his wake a death toll so staggering that the actual number of victims may never be known . . .

For the first time, here is the true story of Henry Lee Lucas's confessions of murder, rape, and mutilation – from the victims he chose by chance, to his equally depraved partner Ottis Toole and his young niece, Becky, who found love and death in Lucas's arms. This startling book examines Lucas's cross-country spree that ended with his arrest in Texas and the gruesome legacy that began when his confessions led Texas Rangers to buried human remains. The investigation became even more bizarre when Lucas began confessing to crimes he *didn't* commit – and when a D.A. from Waco claimed that the diabolical killer was entirely innocent.

DERANGED

Harold Schechter

THE SHOCKING TRUE STORY OF A FIENDISH KILLER

In May 1928 a kindly old man came to the door of the Budd family home in New York City. A few days later he persuaded Mr and Mrs Budd to let him take their adorable little girl Grace to a birthday party. The Budds agreed. They never saw Grace again. For the harmless white haired visitor to whom they entrusted their child was in reality a monster.

Six years later, after a relentless search by a New York detective and nationwide press coverage, the mystery of Grace Budd's disappearance was finally solved – and an unparalleled crime of horror revealed. What Albert Fish did to Grace Budd and perhaps fifteen other young children went beyond every parent's worst nightmare. And he did it in a way that caused experts to pronounce him the most deranged human being they had ever seen.

Warner Books now offers an exciting range of quality titles by both established and new authors which can be ordered from the following address:

Little Brown and Company (UK) Limited,
P.O. Box 11,
Falmouth,
Cornwall TR10 9EN.

Alternatively you may fax your order to the above address. Fax No. 0326 376423.

Payments can be made as follows: cheque, postal order (payable to Little, Brown and Company) or by credit cards, Visa/Access. Do not send cash or currency. UK customers and B.F.P.O. please allow £1.00 for postage and packing for the first book, plus 50p for the second book, plus 30p for each additional book up to a maximum charge of £3.00 (7 books plus).

Overseas customers including Ireland, please allow £2.00 for the first book plus £1.00 for the second book, plus 50p for each additional book.

NAME(Block Letters) ....

ADDRESS..

....

☐ I enclose my remittance for _____

☐ I wish to pay by Access/Visa Card

Number ☐☐☐☐☐☐☐☐☐☐☐☐☐☐☐☐

Card Expiry Date ☐☐☐☐